WITHDRAWN

Pork Barrel Politics

Pork Barrel Politics

*How Government Spending
Determines Elections in a
Polarized Era*

ANDREW H. SIDMAN

COLUMBIA UNIVERSITY PRESS
New York

Columbia University Press
Publishers Since 1893
New York   Chichester, West Sussex
cup.columbia.edu
Copyright © 2019 Columbia University Press

Library of Congress Cataloging-in-Publication Data
Names: Sidman, Andrew H., author.
Title: Pork barrel politics : how government spending determines elections
in a polarized era / Andrew H. Sidman.
Description: New York : Columbia University Press, 2019. |
Includes bibliographical references and index.
Identifiers: LCCN 2018058411| ISBN 9780231193580 (cloth : alk. paper) |
ISBN 9780231193597 (pbk. : alk. paper) | ISBN 9780231550406 (e-book)
Subjects: LCSH: United States. Congress—Elections. |
United States. Congress—Appropriations and expenditures. |
Government spending policy—United States. |
Polarization (Social sciences)—Political aspects—United States.
Classification: LCC JK1976 .S58 2019 | DDC 324.973—dc23
LC record available at https://lccn.loc.gov/2018058411

Columbia University Press books are printed
on permanent and durable acid-free paper.

Printed in the United States of America

Cover image: Getty Images © Chee Siong Teh/EyeEm

For Barbara and Jerry

Contents

Contents

Acknowledgments

THE GENESIS OF THIS BOOK stretches back far further than the three years it took to research and write it to a dissertation defended more than a decade ago. That work, also on the pork barrel and House elections, was written several years too early. Partisan effects of the pork barrel were my emphasis there, as was an ideological basis for these effects. While I believe the dissertation was well written, hindsight has shown me that the empirical examination was too narrow and my sense of the importance of developing political trends too underdeveloped. In 2006, as I researched my dissertation, the scholarly world was expanding our knowledge about the polarization that now firmly grips American political life. My academic life after defense would be consumed by other projects, but I would return to the pork barrel from time to time. Through some of this research, through teaching classes on public opinion and voting, and in trying to make sense of American politics over the past several years, I found myself engrossed in this literature on polarization. Ideas built around what I had read about the historical pork barrel and contemporary accounts of the electoral effects of distributive politics began to take concrete shape. The result is an argument that places the pork barrel in what I believe is its correct context in American politics— as an issue. As with any issue, voters develop meaningful preferences over the pork barrel and, I argue, these preferences are based in ideology.

Polarization has largely been defined, in both elites and the mass public, by partisan ideological sorting, increased ideological consistency, and intense partisan behavior. The pork barrel provokes stronger ideological reactions because *everything* provokes stronger ideological reactions. The partisan effects of the pork barrel, so inconsistent throughout much of the literature, are sharply focused in an era described by some observers as the most polarized since the end of the Civil War.

As many authors before me have recognized, the completion of any work, especially a book, is nearly impossible without help. This work is the product of more than three years of research, three years that have been filled with personal and professional happenings that give life meaning but make it difficult to sit down and write. I am grateful for all of the help I received getting these ideas onto the printed page. Given the development of this work from my aforementioned dissertation, I am indebted to the members of my dissertation committee: my adviser Scott Basinger, René Lindstädt, Shana Rose, and Jeffrey Segal. I returned regularly to their feedback in the early stages of this research, and I am grateful for their insights as the work progressed. Various incarnations of the ideas set forth here have been presented in a number of forums and academic conferences. I thank the many participants and discussants who have given me feedback on my work, especially Kenneth Bickers, Steven Greene, Peter Hanson, and Sean Theriault. I am especially thankful for Jeff Cohen and Maxwell Mak, one my mentor and guide in this profession and the other my longtime colleague and coauthor. Both have been good friends and have provided great feedback on my thoughts and ideas.

I am also grateful for the assistance of my editor at Columbia University Press, Stephen Wesley. He efficiently and expertly guided me through the review process, securing comments from two anonymous reviewers, to whom I also give thanks, that greatly improved this work. Thanks are also due to Kathryn Jorge at Columbia University Press, Ben Kolstad at Cenveo Publisher Services, and their respective teams for the excellent copyediting and typesetting of my manuscript. In addition to those in the broader academic world, I received lots of support from my home institution, including funding for this work that was provided by a grant from the Office for the Advancement of Research at John Jay College.

Last, but certainly not least, all of my endeavors have benefited more than I could recount here from a wonderfully supportive family. My wife, Nicole, has been more than I deserve in every way, and I doubt I could have completed this work without her support. My children, Lily and James, have been endless sources of joy and needed distractions. I am thankful for my in-laws, Donna (mother), Camille (grandmother), and Kristin (sister), for all of their help, giving me more time to write. Finally, I am grateful for my parents, Barbara and Jerry. They were amazing parents, the fiercest advocates of my work, and they devoted their all to my education. It is to them that this book is dedicated.

Pork Barrel Politics

1

Incumbents and Pork Barrel Politics

ON MARCH 10, 2010, House Appropriations Committee chair David Obey, a Democrat, proclaimed that the Appropriation Committee would not consider any earmarks directed to for-profit companies requested for the 2011 budget. In a remarkable step, House Republicans decided the following day to ban earmark requests from their conference altogether (Clarke and Epstein 2010).[1] Attacks on government spending, both large and small, would not stop there. Passed as part of the Budget Control Act of 2011, automatic, widespread spending cuts, known more familiarly as sequestration, took effect March 1, 2013. While sequestration resulted from bipartisan compromise, support for its continuation rested almost entirely within the Republican Party, and more particularly within members of Congress associated with the Tea Party. Closer to the hearts of many in my discipline, 2013 is also notable as the year Senator Tom Coburn, a Republican, briefly succeeded in his four-year quest to severely limit funding for political science research through the National Science Foundation. These three episodes have in common Republican-initiated or Republican-supported cuts to federal distributive spending. Empirical examinations of the pork barrel have asserted for two decades that the fiscally conservative, and Republicans generally, receive little to no electoral benefit from this type of spending. Why, then, did it take Republicans so long to start addressing it—or, more appropriately, why now?

The quick answer is that the high level of polarization in recent politics is necessary for there to be general, systematic costs of pork barreling for Republicans.

This is not a book about Republicans and the pork barrel, but Republicans do receive more attention in the discussion. The simple reason is that distributive politics has had stronger and more complex relationships with House election outcomes for Republicans than for Democrats in the recent era. In part, this may be due to the lopsided nature of polarization itself: Republicans in Congress have become more extreme than Democrats (Bonica et al. 2015), as have Republican voters (Mann 2015). The first aim of this work is to understand the interplay between the pork barrel and polarization in electoral politics. In all of the work on distributive politics and elections, I have yet to come across a single work that examines the role of polarization. Undoubtedly, this is a consequence of data availability; some of the best data on the pork barrel exist for a period of relatively low polarization. It is only recently, considering the full period for which these data exist, that polarization has exhibited sufficient variation to draw meaningful conclusions about its effects. In studying the relationship between pork, polarization, and House elections, this book advances the study of distributive-electoral politics in two additional ways.

First, this work includes data for a longer period than typical studies. Much of the empirical work on the electoral effects of the pork barrel is limited with respect to the time period studied. Research published throughout the 1990s, for example, considers by necessity a period during which Democrats controlled Congress.[2] Few works have examined a longer period that includes the recent era of Republican control, and fewer still have looked at this relationship in the first decade of the twenty-first century. Those that have done so tend to be single-Congress studies of the impact of earmarks, a very specific type of spending for which high-quality data are available for the 110th Congress.[3] All of the district-level research presented here includes data from 1986 through 2012—a period that saw both parties in control of Congress. This is also a period during which polarization varied from low to high, generally increasing throughout the era. Chapter 3, which includes analyses of aggregate election outcomes, looks at the relationship between polarization and public-works spending over a far longer period, starting from 1876.

The second advancement is attention to the indirect effects of the pork barrel on election outcomes. There has been a lot of work on the direct effects of the pork barrel on election outcomes, but very little on its indirect effects: the way the pork barrel shapes other outcomes of interest leading to the result on Election Day. Securing project and programmatic spending for the district is part of what a representative does, and this behavior shapes the way constituents view their representative and the way strategic actors view the upcoming election. In practically every empirical work on the topic, the dependent variable is some variation of the district-level vote share of the incumbent. A few studies have examined the effects of pork on the entry decisions of experienced challengers. A small number of works have also considered the link between the pork barrel and individual attitudes and, ultimately, voting behavior. Each chapter of this work presents a different facet of the electoral relationship leading up to the final chapter on district-level election outcomes.

In the following chapters, I consider three district-level indirect effects. First, I look at the role of the pork barrel in determining primary competition. Potential candidates are strategic actors. They have been most studied in the context of challenger quality in general elections, but strategic concerns are relevant to challenger entry in primaries as well. Second, general-election challenger experience is analyzed in its own right. Part of my conclusion is that potential candidates with electoral experience are part of the same political system as House incumbents. Many of the latter believe pork barreling to be electorally beneficial, and many of the former likely hold the same view. There is, therefore, a deterrent effect of pork barreling. For primary competition, particularly for Republicans, there is an antideterrent, or what could be called an "encouragement" effect, inviting competition when polarization is high. Because the analysis of primary competition does not consider the experience of challengers, it could be the case that many of these challengers, who are electoral amateurs, do not base their decisions to run on the same assumptions as their experienced counterparts. Considerations of candidate spending comprise the third indirect effect to be discussed. Campaign donors are no less strategic in their decision making, and pork barreling influences their behavior as well.

Returning to the question of "why now," the average representative is sure to have little knowledge of the academic literature on the pork barrel. To be fair to members and their staffs, that literature taken as a whole has been inconsistent regarding the electoral effects of the pork barrel. Studies conducted prior to the publication of Stein and Bickers's (1994a) seminal work on the topic tend to find no systematic relationship at all. Even for Stein and Bickers, the district-level results are weak, and the lynchpin of their individual-level analysis is voter awareness of incumbent activities. Stein and Bickers popularized data from the Federal Assistance Awards Data System, or FAADS. Subsequent work, most of which employs the FAADS data, has been more successful at linking the pork barrel to election outcomes, often conditioning the effects of pork on legislator characteristics such as party or ideology. The argument I offer is that high polarization is necessary to observe general, systematic partisan effects. The pork barrel is not salient as an issue. At higher levels of polarization, however, information about the pork barrel is more likely to correlate with broader attitudes on government spending in an ideologically consistent manner, leading to more easily observed partisan effects. In this way, polarization explains some of the inconsistency in the literature. Research looking only at periods of low polarization tends to find null effects. Studies that cover more recent elections include a period during which polarization is increasing and the pork barrel is having effects that are more consistently partisan.

Work on the electoral effects of the pork barrel necessarily involves several themes relevant to our understanding of the legislative branch and American politics broadly. The study of congressional elections is largely the study of incumbents and the advantages they possess. Especially where the pork barrel is concerned, the analysis is of an activity we expect to be tied to incumbents—for good, as much of the literature has assumed, or for bad, as I will demonstrate in later chapters. I argue that polarization is key to understanding the relationship between particularistic spending and elections. Underlying polarization are party, ideology, and, in the American context, the way these identities and ways of understanding the political world have become more entangled over the past two decades. I turn to each of these themes now.

Incumbents and Reelection

The importance of David Mayhew's (1974) *Congress: The Electoral Connection* to the study of congressional elections cannot be overstated. Its simple and elegant argument is that members are motivated primarily by the electoral goal and that, in achieving this goal, members have distinct advantages over their competitors, through credit claiming, position taking, and advertising. The prevailing view of congressional elections scholars has been that all three of these activities work together to comprise incumbency advantage. To be sure, over the four decades since publication of Mayhew's monumental work, we have observed members of Congress taking positions through their statements and rollcall behavior, securing federal dollars for their states and districts, advertising their positions and distributive activities, and generally winning election by safe margins and at very high rates. This view, however, developed during an important transition in congressional politics. The 1970s and 1980s witnessed relatively low polarization, both in Congress and in the public. Congress, for the first time in U.S. history, opted to regulate campaign finance. These new regulations coincided with a growth in the number of new members less beholden to the institutional power brokers of the past and more single-minded in their pursuit of the electoral goal. This seeming free-for-all does not describe the Congress of today. Congress in the twenty-first century is more polarized than in decades past, mirroring the growing polarization among partisans in the mass public. The institutional power wielded by the committee chairs of an earlier era is held, perhaps even more strongly, by today's party leaders. And while the electoral goal remains paramount, the regularity of "wave" elections signals a much closer relationship between the fortunes of the member and those of the party than existed in the 1970s and 1980s. It is in this context that I question the general consideration of pork barreling as credit claiming.

Mayhew writes, "How much particularized benefits count for at the polls is extraordinarily difficult to say, but it would be hard to find a Congressman who thinks he can afford to wait around until precise information is available. The lore is that they count" (1974, 57). A key assumption of my argument, one that differs from much of the literature, is that the pork barrel is an issue on which significant subsets of the public hold negative opinions. Nearly all of the work on distributive politics starts with a simple assumption based in rational choice theory: constituents prefer receiving more benefits over receiving fewer benefits. The assumption that everyone wants something pervades work on distributive politics, even when much of the empirical work on the intersection between distributive and electoral politics has failed to find that direct link. The effects of distributive benefits in several of these studies are not universal. They are conditioned by factors such as party, ideology, or the type of benefit, recognizing that legislators from different parties tend to benefit from different types of programs. The "more is better" assumption, combined with the observation of these conditional effects, has led to the general conclusion that there is always a systematic benefit of pork barreling, assuming the legislator secures the "right" pork for her party, and rarely, if ever, a cost for other pork. Because voters always want more, regardless of whether the benefits are more traditional grant and direct payment programs or contingent liabilities, this spending is the "stuff" of credit claiming. To the contrary, I argue that the pork barrel is not an apolitical assortment of benefits. Collectively, it is, and always has been, an ideological issue.

Party Politics and Polarization

At around the same time that Mayhew was exploring the electoral motivations of members of Congress, other scholars were investigating a phenomenon that would be called "dealignment," the detachment of large segments of the public from partisan politics, especially in party identification (Abramson 1976; Norpoth and Rusk 1982). This dealignment of the mass public would also occur during a period marked by weak parties in Congress. As late as 1993, Keith Krehbiel was asking "Where's the Party?" and concluding that the political parties exerted a relatively weak influence over behavior in Congress, despite the increasingly homogenous preferences of party members. As I will show in the next chapter, polarization was very low in the 1970s and has increased steadily through the present. The year 1993 was also one year before

6

Republicans would regain control over both chambers of Congress in an election year marked by concerted efforts by Republican leaders to campaign on a national message (Jacobson 1996). Fast-forward to the present, and few would argue against the emergence of party as a powerful motivator of behavior in Congress, with party leaders wielding more influence than in the earlier eras. Increasing ideological homogeneity within the parties and growing divisions between them are the conditions assumed to underlie a shift of institutional power to party leaders (Rohde 1991). Conditional party government, as this theory is called, is caused by the same divisions that define elite polarization. Members of each party in Congress have become increasingly unified around their preferred policy outcomes, while the ideological distance between average members of the parties has grown. This has allowed the parties to put forward clear ideological positions to the electorate and has left little space for compromise on most issues facing the nation (Lee 2009, 2016).

Despite the prevalence of elite polarization, there is a debate over whether we observe these divisions in the mass public. Some would argue, perhaps most famously Fiorina, Abrams, and Pope (2006), that the belief we are a 50–50 nation is a myth. Although our elections may be highly contested and results evenly divided, the preferences of the mass public are less divided and more moderate than our election outcomes make them appear (Ellis and Stimson 2012). On the other side, several scholars have observed clearer signs of mass polarization, especially in the partisan public—those individuals who identify with one of the major parties. While increasing partisan rancor in the mass public is a cause for concern (Mason 2015), more relevant to this work is the closer relationship between ideology and party identification (Abramowitz and Saunders 2008; Levendusky 2009). Whether the public as a whole remains moderate and shares preferences on most issues is debatable. The subset of partisans, however, have become more willing to adopt the preferred ideological positions of their chosen party and have become far more ideologically consistent across issues than in the past (Abramowitz 2015). Jacobson (2015) notes that the electorate in 2012 was more polarized than in any election for which we have survey data. In preferences and identification, Democrats were more likely to be liberal, Republicans were more likely to be conservative, and both sets of partisans, by virtue member requests for project funding have disappeared.[4] They are, however, a small part of a vast system of what the federal government generally calls "domestic assistance" and what the academic literature labels "distributive benefits." The role of the member in this process is less about adding particular projects to regular appropriations or omnibus spending bills and more about budgetary authority over federal agencies and facilitating or assisting interested parties in securing federal money. Federal projects and grant assistance comprise a significant share of the casework done by members and their staffs (Johannes 1983a).

The *Catalog of Federal Domestic Assistance* (Executive Office 2012), which lists the programs that comprise much of the data on distributive benefits, includes several types of assistance pertinent here. Although there are many ways to classify these programs, this research requires measures of the pork barrel that comport with partisan and, more importantly, ideological preferences. The core of my argument is that the pork barrel has systematic partisan effects only when high levels of polarization activate ideological sentiment toward these types of spending. One could, for example, distinguish pork by perceived partisan preferences for the target of the spending. The next chapter includes extensive discussion of defense and national security spending as a measure of "Republican" pork. While there is support in the literature (and basic attention to politics) for Republican preferences for defense spending, recent work suggests that the distribution of defense pork is more complex and may not follow typical partisan or ideological patterns (Thorpe 2014). A potentially more useful way to distinguish measures of pork for this research is the distinction between programs that make direct payments to other levels of government or private actors and contingent liability programs.

"Distributive spending," as such pork will be referred to here, includes four types of assistance. Formula grants are allocations of funds to states or their subdivisions, which are then further distributed by those government actors. Project grants supply funding for specific projects for fixed periods. The other two types are payments made directly to private actors, either requiring a particular performance by the actor or not. "Contingent liabilities" include three types of assistance. Direct loans are those made directly by a federal agency. Guaranteed loan programs indemnify private lenders against default. These programs typically allow private lenders to offer more favorable terms to prospective borrowers. Insurance programs provide coverage against loss, either directly from the federal government or through private providers.

The basic difference between distributive spending and contingent liabilities is that direct payment and grant programs represent what could be considered typical discretionary government spending, whereas contingent liability programs make outlays where there is an expectation of repayment (loans) or when the beneficiary has suffered a loss (insurance). The distinction is an important one because of the role that ideology is expected to play in understanding the interplay between the pork barrel and polarization in House elections. In a general sense, it is expected that conservatives oppose most forms of government spending and liberals support such spending. Considering distributive spending and contingent liabilities separately, the literature has referred to the former as "Democratic pork" and the latter as "Republican pork" (Bickers and Stein 2000). This goes beyond mere preference and is entangled with the values feeding each ideological disposition. Direct payment and grant programs represent positive government—government using the resources of citizens to promote positive societal ends. Whether it is the classic public-works infrastructure project or a National Science Foundation research grant, government is directing monetary resources to programs that are intended to benefit society. This type of spending, which sees government as equalizer, collecting taxes and distributing that revenue to where it will do "good," comports with the general liberal disposition toward equality of outcomes. Contingent liabilities, on the other hand, provide a safety net of sorts for private behavior. Loans to small businesses or homebuyers, or crop and bank-deposit insurance, are examples of government supporting the conditions for private enterprise. As noted earlier, loans need to be repaid and insurance covers losses. These programs, therefore, do not represent typical government spending. Instead, they more closely match the value orientation of modern conservatism, emphasizing equality of opportunity. Government programs are used to provide a more level playing field for private actors, but those actors still succeed or fail by their own merit. The business owner receiving a loan from the Small Business Administration will hopefully use those resources to become more profitable. The loan, however, needs to be repaid whether the business thrives or falters.

An Issue-Based Theory of the Pork Barrel and Elections

The pork barrel is rarely an issue that is salient enough to generate significant reaction from the electorate. At the very least, it is never volunteered by survey respondents when asked what is the most important issue facing the nation. It is more likely that the pork barrel contributes to people's affect toward government spending, which is a broad issue of which people are more cognizant. On one side, voters could see the pork barrel as part of "good" government, directing its resources to projects and programs that benefit people. This is arguably truest among citizens who benefit directly from this spending, such as the local nonprofit receiving a federal grant. Consider this quote from an article describing two viewing parties in Buffalo, New York, watching the 2016 Democratic presidential debate held in Brooklyn on April 14:

> "Right down the street there, the medical campus would not be there today if it wasn't for Congressman [Brian] Higgins and Secretary Clinton," said Jeremy Zellner, chairman of the Erie County Democratic Committee, as he gestured toward the cluster of buildings that includes Roswell, and other medical research and education facilities. The growth of the medical campus has helped revitalize the Rust Belt city, which Clinton pointed out during her visit to Buffalo last week. (Bowman 2016)

Interestingly, the article had nothing to do with distributive politics. Yet, in recounting reasons why Secretary Hillary Clinton would be a better president than Senator Bernie Sanders, Mr. Zellner, certainly a more sophisticated observer of politics owing to his political position, noted Clinton's role as a U.S. senator in securing federal money for the city. It is also notable that Mr. Zellner included Representative Brian Higgins, elected in 2004, in his kudos. As chair of the Erie County Democratic Committee, Mr. Zellner is a member of the political elite, and this brief anecdote highlights two of the ways average voters can come to credit their representatives for pork barreling: by elected officials touting their activities, as Secretary Clinton did, and by local opinion leaders like Mr. Zellner disseminating that message. This view illustrates the assumption that voters generally prefer that their districts receive a share of these monies.

On the other side, the pork barrel is seen as wasteful spending, from which the average citizen derives no benefit. At its worst, the pork barrel is emblematic of the rigged game of government, with resources going toward those with access at the expense of those without. In his 1974 book, *Pork Barrel Politics*, John Ferejohn quotes the autobiography of Representative Joe Martin, a Republican from Massachusetts, on the political perils of pork barreling:

> When I was first elected to Congress . . . I fell heir to the old Taunton River issue. For a hundred years my district had been interested in having the river widened and deepened to make it navigable for steamers.
>
> Where my predecessors had failed I got the necessary legislation through Congress, only to find it the biggest issue raised against me in the next election. The railroads were angry because it threatened them with new competition. The gas company people were furious because they feared that they would be put to great expense removing their pipes from the river bed. The owners of a large stove company at Taunton were frantic lest the widening of the river weaken the foundation of their factory. *And to top it off many of the voters were suspicious that I, who would become a veritable symbol of economy in government, was a big spender* [emphasis added]. (Martin 1960, quoted in Ferejohn 1974, 51)

Overall, distributive spending exists as an issue (or set of issues) on which different individuals develop a variety of meaningful attitudes, generally being either supportive of or opposed to such spending. Furthermore, the individual's political predispositions, primarily ideology, determine those attitudes. The pork barrel, however, is not a "normal" issue; more precisely, it is part of the more general issues of government spending and the appropriate role of government and lacks the salience of those larger issue domains. Polarization has two effects that are important here. First, in a polarized environment, information about the pork barrel becomes more relevant to general attitudes on government spending. Polarization is assumed to intensify ideological divisions; make issues on which clear ideological disagreements exist, such as government spending, more salient; and strengthen the links between evaluations, behavior, and information relevant to those issues, such as information on the distributive activities of representatives.

Second, in this most recent era, we have observed polarization among elected officials (elite polarization) and partisan polarization among the mass public. This second type, coinciding with what the literature calls sorting, is characterized by increasing partisan ideological consistency. Simply, more Democrats have become liberal and more Republicans have become conservative in the mass public. Returning to House elections and the pork barrel, in an era of low polarization, both Democratic and Republican representatives will likely have a significant part of their electoral constituency holding liberal preferences over government spending generally and the pork barrel specifically. Both will have also constituents preferring less spending. As polarization increases and partisan identifiers begin to sort, the typical Republican representative with a predominantly Republican electoral constituency will face voters who increasingly hold conservative preferences on spending. Likewise, the typical Democratic representative will face voters who increasingly hold liberal preferences. Thus, it is not until polarization is high that we would observe general, systematic electoral benefits and costs from pork barreling.

When certain types of pork barreling can be electorally harmful, there is a question of why members of Congress work to secure any awards that have the potential to cost them votes. This question is explored in greater detail in the next chapter. It is important to note here, however, that part of the decision calculus of members includes an assessment of how constituents will react to a particular action and the likelihood that potential voters will actually learn about the action (Arnold 1990). There is at least one constituent, or group of constituents, that will laud the distributive action of the member: the beneficiary of federal funding. Even if the broader constituency opposes that spending, members likely assume that the probability of voters' learning about the spending and translating that information into disapproval of the member is so low as to be practically nonexistent. I assume this is particularly the case in a low-polarization environment, where I have argued that the link between the pork barrel and attitudes on government spending are weaker.[5] The pork barrel, then, exists in the background. Members can reward supporters (or gain new ones) with few repercussions, and party leaders can use pork to build majority coalitions and reward loyalty (Cann and Sidman 2011; Evans 2004). We fail to observe a general, systematic link between overall in-district spending and election outcomes because such a link does not exist. Incumbents benefit in different ways (e.g., through campaign contributions or increases in popularity among particular groups) that make the overall, general effects of pork barrel spending marginal at best and idiosyncratic at worst.

Why, then, do members still engage in this behavior when polarization is on the rise? One answer could be a failure of members and their staffs to update their assumptions. That is, they underestimate the likelihood that information about distributive activities will be received, negatively perceived, and acted on by constituents. Furthermore, over a long period of incumbent safety and success, aided significantly by gerrymandering, members might take their safety for granted and assume that the potential general-election benefits of pork barreling outweigh the potential costs of turning off the strongest ideologues in their districts. Formation of this flawed assumption is understandable given the complexity with which congressional elections operate. There can be any number of reasons to explain an incumbent's suffering an electoral cost, whether a decrease in vote share from previous elections or even a loss. Singling out distributive activities is likely to be impossible in all but a very small number of cases, and their effects are, as stated earlier, modest at best. What is lost in this complexity, however, is that distributive politics can have effects beyond those directly on the incumbent's vote share on Election Day. Distributive benefits affect primary competition, the emergence of experienced challengers, and fund-raising by both candidates. All of these are indirect effects of the pork barrel, working through factors that are highly determinative of election results.

Plan for the Book

My argument begins with the premises that pork barrel spending is an ideologically divisive issue, that polarization can increase the salience of the pork barrel to voters and other actors, and that individual attitudes regarding government spending affect candidate preferences. The next three chapters present support for these assumptions. Chapter 2 investigates the distribution of different types of pork barrel spending as conditioned by polarization. After presenting the measures of the pork barrel and polarization used throughout the book, I examine various theoretical expectations for the distribution of pork, finding that polarization plays an important role in determining how much pork of different types legislators pursue. Chapter 3 discusses my issue-based theory of distributive-electoral politics in its historical context. Evidence is presented in the form of an aggregate analysis of public-works spending and House election outcomes from 1876 through 2012. The results show that public-works spending has had the expected partisan effects on incumbent vote share, but only as polarization increases. Chapter 4 examines the links between the pork barrel and mass attitudes on government spending. Analyses of American National Election Studies data show that distributive spending is linked to the identification of government spending as a national problem. More importantly, when polarization is high, there are significant effects of distributive spending on overall government spending preferences. The chapter concludes with an analysis of voting behavior in several elections from 1986 through 2012. In periods of higher polarization, increasing distributive spending decreases the likelihood of voting for the incumbent among self-identified conservatives.

Having built support for the arguments that polarization conditions the effects of distributive politics and that distributive spending affects individual attitudes and behavior, in the remaining chapters I explore the district-level electoral implications of these findings. Chapter 5 shows that polarization and distributive politics combine to affect primary competition. Chapter 6 considers their impact on general-election challenger quality and campaign fund-raising. Chapter 7 brings all of this district-level work together in an analysis of House election outcomes from 1986 through 2012 and provides a full picture of how the pork barrel has affected incumbent vote share in the most recent era of congressional electoral politics. Across a variety of district-level outcomes, the results are remarkably consistent. When polarization is high, incumbents benefit from securing pork consistent with the ideological preferences of their party's base voters and pay electoral costs for securing pork inconsistent with these preferences. Finally, a conclusion places all of these findings in context and presents my speculations for the future of the pork barrel in congressional politics.

2

Pursuing the Pork Barrel

THE INTRODUCTORY CHAPTER advances my theory that the electoral effects of the pork barrel are conditioned by political polarization. Polarization among elites in Congress and in the mass public has many meaningful consequences for politics and policy making. Polarization is thought to be a primary cause of legislative gridlock, especially during periods of divided government (Binder 1999). Polarization had led to increased levels of anger and activism among partisans both in and out of Congress (Hetherington 2001; Mason 2015). Gerrymandering, both a potential cause and consequence of polarization, has created safe districts that promote extremity from congressional candidates. The relative general-election safety that candidates enjoy has led to a decrease in substantive coverage of House campaigns (Hayes and Lawless 2015). Where the media are concerned, we see polarization buoyed not just by partisan media outlets, but by all media outlets (Arceneaux and Johnson 2015). When the story, regardless of the source, is how polarized our politics have become, it is hard for the attentive public not to follow their own partisan cues. This environment becomes the backdrop against which legislators are making policy choices, including decisions on the pork barrel.

The theory, as I have described it, is that polarization stimulates ideological reactions from the public. In the minds of voters, the pork barrel becomes more interwoven with federal spending, a broad issue area with clear ideological underpinnings. Polarization is defined by the ideological separation of the parties and, through nonstop partisan battling, increased clarity in each party's ideological positions. With gerrymandering providing significant partisan homogeneity in most House districts, incumbents ignore the ideologues among their constituents at their own peril. My argument is that incumbents are rewarded for securing federal benefits that are consistent with the ideological preferences of their constituents and are punished for securing benefits counter to these preferences. While the remaining chapters comprising the bulk of this work consider pork as an independent variable, it is worth considering whether legislators, who are surely cognizant of these developments, adjust their pork barreling behavior. The presentation in this chapter has two goals. The first, alluded to in the introductory chapter, is to identify measures of the pork barrel that are based in ideological preferences. There, I suggested three possible measures: distributive spending, which encompasses direct payment and grant programs; contingent liabilities, which are loan and insurance programs; and defense pork. From a popular perspective, few issue areas in the domain of government spending evoke partisan reactions similar to spending on defense and national security. The second goal is to answer the question of whether polarization has led legislators to pursue the pork that is ideologically consistent with their party label. The consensus among scholars is that the distribution of the pork barrel is affected by politics broadly. Electoral vulnerability, partisan politics, and the relative power of members all factor into which benefits are given to which districts. My analysis adds polarization as another political consideration affecting the pork barrel.

Explanations for the Distribution of the Federal Pork Barrel

Considering the distribution of benefits and the observation that almost all districts do indeed receive some benefits, much of the theoretical work has focused on explaining why the equilibrium outcome is usually closer to universalism. All of these explanations formalize the reception of benefits as a multiplayer game. In order for a given project to pass and benefits to be distributed, the program needs a minimum winning coalition (MWC), which will vary in size for a given set of conditions. In general, the MWC can range from a simple majority, which is needed to pass the legislation that initiates the spending, to universalism, in which all members must be part of the winning coalition. Shepsle and Weingast (1981), for example, state that under pure majority rule, the outcome should be majoritarian, but uncertainty surrounding which representatives will comprise the MWC generates outcomes closer to universalism. Benefits are assumed to have important electoral consequences and further assumed to be generally preferred by voters (Anagnoson 1982; Niou and Ordeshook 1985); thus, every legislator is compelled to secure at least some benefits. To ensure they are not left out of current or future coalitions, representatives are often willing to increase the size of coalitions, even if it means receiving a smaller share of benefits. Empirically, Wilson (1986) finds support for this proposition in river and harbor legislation between 1889 and 1913. Hamman (1993) also finds that universalism results as legislators seek support for particular subsets of policy areas; the individual subsets are not distributed universally, but considering the area as a whole (mass transportation programs), universalism develops as beneficiaries from each subset support one another. Universalism can also result from distortion in the costs and benefits of projects—specifically, the diffuse nature of costs and the concentration of benefits—assuming that legislators seek projects in which their reelection constituencies are beneficiaries (Weingast, Shepsle, and Johnsen 1981).

The electoral motivation for pork barreling receives empirical support from the work that finds the distribution of benefits skewed toward electorally vulnerable members. A number of recent studies that have taken advantage of changes to rules governing earmark requests have found that both the number and the value of earmarks tend to increase as the previous vote share of the incumbent decreases (Engstrom and Vanberg 2010; Lazarus 2009, 2010; Lazarus and Steigerwalt 2009). Grimmer (2013) adds that members who represent safe districts tend to rely less on pork barreling and more on position taking. Safe districts, reflecting a high level of partisan homogeneity, see representatives more concerned with the ideological content of policy, whereas incumbents from marginal districts

McCubbins 1993; Adler 2002). This is certainly true of committees that focus on specific arenas, such as agricultural policy.[1] To the extent that there is a relationship between committee membership, at least on committees that represent particular constituency interests, and constituency demand for legislative outputs, we can also emphasize the importance of constituents to legislative outputs. The committee system may also provide increased insulation for distributive politics from the eyes of the general public. Putting all of these features together, the committee system is often identified as an important factor in the distribution of benefits (Adler 2002; Alvarez and Saving 1997a; Bertelli and Grose 2009; Rundquist, Lee, and Rhee 1996). The influence of committee membership is broadly supported; several works have looked specifically at defense-related appropriations and noted the skewing of benefits toward localities with representation on the relevant committees. Hird (1991) found this effect for the distribution of projects by the Army Corps of Engineers, noting that party and ideology played a minimal role in the distribution of benefits. Rundquist, Lee, and Rhee (1996), looking at defense contracts, reached a similar conclusion. Thorpe (2014) reported positive relationships between Defense Committee membership and defense subcontract locations and support for defense expenditures. In a classic study on this topic, Goss (1972) found support for constituency interests' leading to committee membership—specifically, military-base employment in the district leading to membership on defense-related committees—but committee membership did not necessarily lead to greater employment on bases in those districts.

Committees remain important to the legislative work of Congress. Research over the past two decades, however, has placed a strong emphasis on the role of party in the organization and behavior of Congress (Rohde 1991; Cox and McCubbins 1993; McCarty, Poole, and Rosenthal 2001; Snyder and Groseclose 2000, 2001). There is evidence of an expanded role for party leaders in legislative outputs (Sinclair 1995), both directly and in the composition of committees (Cox and McCubbins 1993). Committee chairs are members of the majority party, and the majority party naturally enjoys a majority of the seats on nearly all committees; thus, even if members are committee-focused, they must prefer electoral success for their party as opposed to failure. Aldrich and Rohde (1997, 2005) note that partisan conditions in Congress over recent decades have caused an expansion of party power.[2] Given the increase in party strength and the need for coalition building, there should be a substantial influence of party over the distribution of benefits. Stronger parties come with a price, however, where the concerns of the individual representative are concerned. Members who do not remain loyal to the party coalition risk receiving fewer benefits, given the control that party can assert over committee and floor action in the House (Cann and Sidman 2011). Further, stronger, more polarized parties can lessen the importance of the "personal" vote central to theories of distributive politics (Primo and Snyder 2010). Some commentators have noted, however, that even strong parties will afford their members leeway to pursue their particularistic agenda, even without the full support of the party (Cox and McCubbins 1993).

Parties make natural coalitions among members and are seen as a solution to collective-action problems in general (Aldrich 1995). This is especially true in periods of increased party strength (Aldrich and Rohde 1997, 2005; Rohde 1991). During such periods, we would expect party leaders to exert more control over legislative processes in general and distributive policies in particular, with members of the majority party receiving a greater share of distributive benefits. Levitt and Snyder (1995) found that between 1984 and 1990, districts received more benefits as they became more Democratic in their voting behavior. Bickers and Stein (2000) also found party effects, reporting that after taking majorities in both the House and the Senate, Republicans significantly decreased spending on direct payment programs[3] while increasing the amount spent on contingent liability programs. Similarly, Berry, Burden, and Howell (2010a) found that changes in the strength of the majority party affect the life span of federal programs, with programs more likely to undergo modification or be killed as the party that supports them loses power. Several works cited earlier, as well as others, that examine the distribution of earmarks also note a partisan bias (Balla et al. 2002; Engstrom and Vanberg 2010; Lazarus 2009, 2010; Lazarus and Steigerwalt 2009). Evans (1994, 2004) and Cann and Sidman (2011) place party leaders at the forefront, concluding that leaders use their influence over the pork barrel to build support for policy and encourage party-building activities (e.g., contributing to the campaigns of copartisans).

While legislative behavior is central to distributive outcomes, the distribution of pork is not only affected by the actions of Congress. As an important player in the legislative process and as head of the executive branch, the president, too, has ample opportunities to pork barrel. The programs that comprise the pork barrel are created and funded through legislation. Through the president's responsibility to recommend legislation, authority over budget proposals, and ability to veto, the president can affect the creation, modification, and funding of federal programs (Berry, Burden, and Howell 2010b; Kiewiet and McCubbins 1988; McCarty 2000). Several works suggest an election-related motivation for presidential pork barreling, although there is some debate over presidential strategy in this regard. Larcinese, Rizzo, and Testa (2006) found that outlays are more likely to go to states that have been more supportive of the president in past elections, including midterm elections. Pork barreling, by their analysis, is used to reward past electoral support and not necessarily to gain support in competitive states. This conclusion stands in contrast to that of Kriner and Reeves (2015), who found that presidents target federal grants both to states in which the president's party is strong and to swing states. This is even the case for disaster declarations, which have significant budgetary implications and are more likely in swing and core support states during presidential election years (Kriner and Reeves 2015). In other work, Kriner and Reeves (2012) build the logic of targeting swing states, finding that the vote share of incumbent presidents and successor candidates increases in counties receiving more federal spending. This is contingent on voters' being able to credit a single party (the president's party) for securing the benefits. This is more likely the case when those counties are represented by copartisans and supporters of the president, which itself is predictive of receiving federal spending (Berry, Burden, and Howell 2010b; Hamman and Cohen 1997). Beyond the president, the heads of the federal departments and agencies that administer this spending appear able to influence its distribution. States whose senators are ideologically proximate to the Secretary of Labor are more likely to receive grants from the Department of Labor, for example, and ideological proximity to the Secretary of Defense is a predictor of defense contracts (Bertelli and Grose 2009).

Clearly, the distribution of pork is subject to political manipulation despite the predictions of universalism. Partisan control over Congress affects how much is spent on different types of programs and the life spans of those programs. Beyond partisan preferences, there is likely a majority-party bias in the distribution of the federal pork barrel. Committee members appear more than able to direct federal spending on the programs they oversee to their constituents. Given the president's control over the executive branch, we also see the president's preferences affecting federal programmatic spending. The rationale offered in much of the literature and the context in which some of these conclusions are drawn is electoral. Political actors across the spectrum are assumed to engage in pork barreling for its effects on elections. As the steady rise of polarization has injected partisan politics into nearly every policy question, and as congressional incumbents find themselves facing voters who are increasingly ideological, the question examined here is whether polarization has led legislators to pursue pork more consistent with the perceived ideological preferences of their constituents. That polarization may affect the distribution of federal spending by virtue of the more ideological character of policy makers and their constituents is an implication of Hirano, Snyder, and Ting (2009). They argue that the existence of primaries in homogenously partisan districts will lead candidates to promise benefits targeted toward the more extreme constituents who vote in primaries. Beyond the effects of general-election constituencies, which already have a distinct partisan leaning, the distribution of pork may also reflect the extreme preferences of these more attentive and engaged primary voters. Thus, as polarization increases, Democrats should be promising (and securing) pork that is increasingly liberal and Republicans should be promising pork that is increasingly conservative.

Data and Measures

The dependent variables are the three measures of the pork barrel, introduced in the first chapter and described in the next subsection.[4] The models are estimated using ordinary least squares with robust standard errors. Separate models are estimated for Democratic and Republican districts, leading to the presentation of six sets of results in the next section. Pork is modeled as a function of polarization, legislator and district ideology, and control variables, all of which are described in the following paragraphs. Data from which the dependent variables are constructed are available beginning with the 98th Congress (1983–1984). The dependent variables, two of which are used as independent variables in chapters 4 through 7, are differenced by congress. The analyses, therefore, are of House districts from the 99th Congress (1985–1986) to the 112th Congress (2011–2012).

Measures of the Pork Barrel

At the district level, in common with most modern studies of distributive benefits, I employ data from the Federal Assistance Awards Data System (FAADS). Much of the literature has debated the best way to measure the pork barrel, attempting to strike a balance between inclusion of the right types of spending and measuring pork in a way that is relevant to election outcomes. Several works measure the pork barrel using only "new" awards and spending, whereas I use the total amount, which includes "continuing" awards and spending. The basic argument offered in the literature is that members of Congress will only get credit for what they deliver, hence only what is new. Continuing projects may have been awarded during the tenure of a former member and have no impact on the electoral fortunes of the current representative. Although this could be the case for some awards, I argue that it fails to recognize the reality of tenure among representatives, who tend to represent their districts for long periods. Also, purging the FAADS data of continuation funding is likely to significantly undercount the spending and awards that are attributable to the incumbent. As an extreme example, consider this National Science Foundation grant,[5] awarded to my academic home, John Jay College of Criminal Justice, to fund a STEM program. The award was for a total of $600,000, recorded as two outlays in FAADS. The first of these, the "new" outlay, was $150,000, bearing an action date of March 3, 2009. The second, in the amount of $450,000, is filed as continuation funding, bearing an action date of August 25, 2009, less than six months later.

To the extent that Representative Jerrold Nadler would receive any electoral benefit, using just new funding in a measure of pork means including only the initial outlay of $150,000. Total funding, which I use, includes both outlays. To the extent that voters and other actors prioritize recent action in their decision making, the measures of pork included here are differenced; specifically, I measure pork as the difference in the natural log of spending (or awards, as discussed below) between the current and previous congresses.

The introductory chapter noted that there are different ways to categorize these programs. In this chapter, I consider the three measures of the pork barrel discussed there, each theoretically based in the ideological preferences central to my argument. The first measure I refer to as "distributive spending." It is measured as the congress-difference in the natural log of all spending in the district listed in FAADS, measured in constant 2009 dollars. This is primarily the spending on direct payment and grant programs assumed to be preferred by liberals. The second measure, called "contingent liabilities" throughout this book, refers to the insurance and loan programs assumed to be preferred by conservatives. In these programs, the dollar amount may matter less than the existence of a beneficiary, given the difference in the meaning of spending on these programs (a loan amount to be repaid or a payment to cover a loss). Consistent with the existing literature, therefore, I measure these programs using the number of awards instead the amount of spending. Thus, the second district-level measure of the pork barrel used here is the congress-difference in the natural log of contingent liability awards in the district. The third measure, which is also assumed to be preferred by conservatives and therefore beneficial to Republican incumbents, is "defense pork." Defense pork is measured as the congress-difference in spending included in FAADS by the Department of Defense and, starting in 2003, the Department of Homeland Security. Starting in chapter 4, I use only the measures of distributive spending and contingent liability awards in the analyses. Although defense spending clearly has particular partisan support, the distribution of defense pork and its electoral effects do not reflect the ideological divisions important to my polarization-based theory in the same, clear ways that distributive spending and contingent liability awards do. These issues are discussed in greater detail toward the end of this chapter.

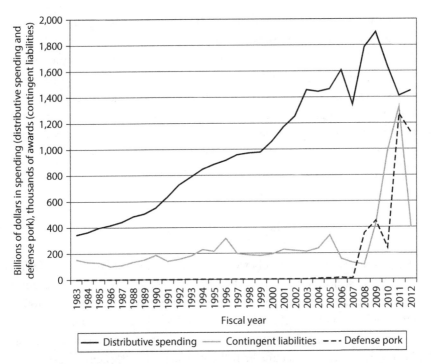

FIGURE 2.1 **Growth of the pork barrel over time**
Curves depict annual total spending or awards for the three measures of the pork barrel presented in this chapter. Distributive spending and defense pork are measured in billions of dollars (constant 2009 dollars). Contingent liabilities are measured in thousands of awards. *Source*: U.S. Bureau of the Census (n.d.), U.S. Bureau of Fiscal Service (2019).

Figure 2.1 shows annual federal allocations for all three measures of pork. Distributive spending and defense pork are measured in billions of dollars. Contingent liabilities are measured in thousands of awards. With few exceptions, distributive spending has steadily increased year after year for most of the period examined here. The trend in contingent liability awards is much flatter until the onset of the Great Recession in 2009 sees a massive increase in loan and insurance awards. One can presume that the federal government filled the gap created by the financial services industry's scaling back of these activities. The small scale of defense pork relative to total distributive spending masks some significant increases during increased use of the military. There is a large bump, for example, coinciding with the Persian Gulf War, and steady growth during the entire War on Terror period. Figure 2.1 shows sharp increases in programmatic defense spending after 2007. A detailed examination of this growth is beyond the scope of this work, but between 2010 and 2012, the period with the largest growth in defense pork, Congress created twenty-six new programs in the Department of Defense and eleven new programs in the Department of Homeland Security. Spending on these new programs is a likely suspect for the rapid increases in defense pork.

Mass Political Polarization

The literature offers a number of ways to measure polarization. Within Congress, scholars have looked, for example, at levels of party unity and ideological divisions between the parties. Given that polarization is expected to condition the effects of pork barreling, an incumbent activity, my preference is for a measure of polarization external to Congress. Where that activity occurs in roll-call votes, it influences measures of polarization based on congressional characteristics. Granted, that influence is probably quite small. Beyond that empirical issue, there is a broader question of which polarization, mass or elite, is more appropriate for testing the theory that polarization conditions the electoral effects of pork. Especially with the focus on elections and, fundamentally, voter responses, I prefer to use a measure of political polarization in the mass public where possible. Work on mass polarization has used indices of survey responses to issue-oriented items as measures (Abramowitz and Saunders 2008; Mason 2015). I follow a similar strategy here.

The individual and district-level analyses throughout this book employ a measure of mass polarization derived from Likert scales of responses to issue-oriented questions in the American National Election Studies (ANES). The first year for which there are enough issue-oriented items from which to build a scale is 1964. Whereas the items ask for issue preferences, collectively the scales are measures of ideological orientation. As unidimensional constructs, an individual's placement on the scale is effectively a measure of how liberal or conservative that person is across several issues. For every year except 2006 and 2010, the cumulative data file (CDF) was used to create the scales. To fill in the missing years, I used data from the 2006 Pilot Study and the 2010 Panel Recontact Study. A scale is created for each year from 1964 through 2012 using standardized versions of the items available.[6] The Cronbach's α for each year is presented in figure 2.2. As a measure of scale quality, the values of α show that the items included are better measures of preferences in certain years than in others. In particular, the scales are better in presidential election years (with a mean difference in α of 0.086) and better in the years included in subsequent analyses (the mean α for scales from 1986 through 2012 is 0.089 larger than the mean for 1964 through 1984). For each respondent, the pieces of information relevant to the polarization measure are scale placement and party identification. The final measure of polarization, which varies by election year, is the absolute difference between the mean placement of Democratic identifiers and the mean

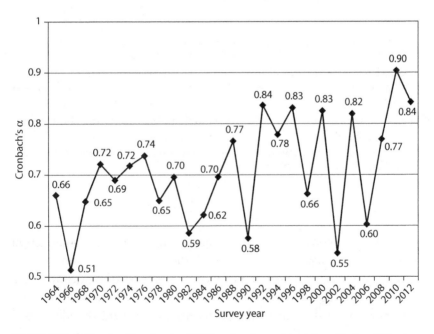

FIGURE 2.2 Cronbach's α for the ANES scales. *Source*: American National Election Studies (2007, 2011, 2015).

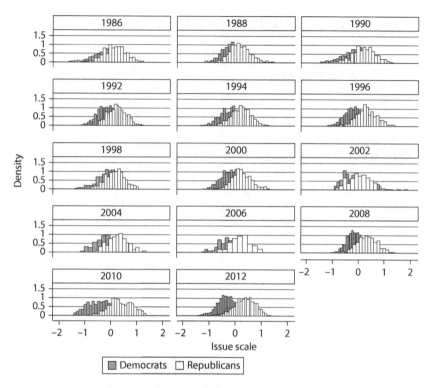

FIGURE 2.3 **Distributions of issue scale by election year**
The graphs depict the distribution of the ANES issue scale for Democratic and Republican identifiers in each election year included in the analyses presented in this chapter and in chapters 4 through 7. Negative values on the horizontal axis denote increasing liberalism. Positive values denote increasing conservatism. Distributions for 1964 through 1984 are available from the author upon request. *Source*: American National Election Studies (2007, 2011, 2015).

placement of Republican identifiers, making it a measure of polarization in the partisan mass public. Figure 2.3 shows the distribution of scale placement—or, in practical terms, ideology—for partisan identifiers for each year included in the individual and district-level analyses. The figure shows a steady drift in the partisan public toward the ideological extremes, corresponding to the increasing polarization many observers have noted over the past decade and a half.

Control Variables

The literature on distributive politics highlights a number of variables expected to affect the distribution of federal particularistic spending. Broadly, ideology, legislator characteristics, electoral vulnerability, and district demand all potentially affect the amount of spending and number of awards received by districts. Beyond these, the progression of time itself can factor into the distribution of pork. These data are pooled, cross-sectional time series. It is almost certainly the case that pork received by a district is a function of what that district has received in the past. Similarly, figure 2.1 implies that significant changes in the amounts of pork occur around the 110th and 111th Congresses.[7] To account for this, the distributive spending and defense pork models control for the natural log of spending in the previous congress. The expectation is that districts that received more spending in the previous congress will receive less in the current congress. Additionally, the contingent liabilities models include a dummy variable for the 111th Congress, and the defense pork models include dummies for the 110th and 111th Congresses, to control for the large increases in those periods. I now turn the discussion to the remaining control variables.

Party is more likely than ideology to be identified as a factor in the distribution of benefits. Party is included implicitly through the estimation of pork on partisan subsamples of the data. Yet even within parties, ideology may be important to the distribution of benefits. Where the measures of pork used here are assumed to appeal to different ideological preferences, it is expected that legislator ideology—measured using the first dimension of DW-NOMINATE scores (McCarty, Poole, and Rosenthal 1997), which increases with conservatism—is negatively related to distributive spending and positively related to contingent liabilities and defense pork. I expect the opposite for district liberalism, which is measured as the proportion of the two-party vote received by the Democratic presidential nominee in the most recent election. More support for the Democratic candidate should be indicative of a more liberal electorate (Erikson and Wright 1980), which should in turn indicate preferences for distributive spending and against contingent liabilities and defense pork.

The literature on the distribution of pork identifies the importance of electoral vulnerability. I include three measures of vulnerability in the pork models. First is the incumbent's share of the two-party vote in the previous election. Vulnerability would be indicated by a smaller share of the vote. An increase in vote share is expected to cause a decrease in all three measures of the pork barrel. Second is the spending gap in the last election, measured as the log of challenger spending minus the log of incumbent spending. Increases here signify an increase in challenger spending relative to incumbent spending. Incumbents facing well-financed challengers tend to be more vulnerable, increasing the incumbent's demand for pork barrel spending. Finally, challenger experience in the last election, measured using a dummy variable scored 1 for challengers who have held an elective office, should also indicate a vulnerable incumbent and cause an increase in pork barreling.

Beyond electoral vulnerability, the literature identifies several legislator characteristics related to the pork barrel. Many of these characteristics address the power that certain members have, giving them the ability to increase their share of the pork barrel. I include dummy variables for the following: (1) serving in a leadership position (defined as Speaker of the House, majority leader, minority leader, majority whip, or minority whip), (2) holding a position of committee chair or ranking minority member on one of the House's standing committees, (3) membership on the House Appropriations Committee, and (4) being a member of the majority party. In addition to these four variables, I control for the seniority of the representative, which is measured as the number of terms served including the current congress. Every additional term served gives a representative more familiarity with the rules of the House, a wider network of fellow members to work with, and possibly power gains within the party. Finally, I control for the party unity score of the member in the previous congress. This is measured as the percentage of times a member votes with her party on conflictual roll-call votes, defined as votes on which at least half of Republicans oppose at least half of Democrats.[8]

District demand for federal benefits comprises the final set of control variables. Some districts, because of their composition, will have a higher demand for distributive benefits than others. This leads representatives of those districts to seek membership on committees that allow them to directly address the preferences of constituents. A representative from a district that contains a large number of farms, for example, would want to be on the Agriculture Committee. Membership here would afford the representative the ability to support programs administered through the Department of Agriculture that are important to residents of his district. Adler (2002) empirically examined district demand for benefits, but analyzed benefits separately by congressional committees. The findings were as expected: a higher percentage of individuals living in rural farming areas, for example, led to that district's receiving more agriculture benefits. The difficulty that arises in studying distributive benefits generally is ascertaining which constituency characteristics lead to greater levels of overall funding. For the sake of expediency, I simply control for as many population characteristics as feasible. Specifically, I include the percentage of the district population that is over age sixty-four, identifies as black, attends school, is foreign born, is a veteran, or lives in an urban area. Additionally, I control for the employment characteristics of the district population, including the percentage unemployed and the percentages who work in the following areas: construction, finance, government, manufacturing, military, transportation, and wholesale and retail. Finally, I control for the natural log of the district's median income and the natural log of the district's population.[9]

Results

Table 2.1 presents selected results for the six pork models. Coefficients and robust standard errors are presented for polarization, legislator ideology (DW-NOMINATE scores), and district liberalism. I do not present coefficients for the remaining control variables. Rather, the second panel of table 2.1 presents the results of joint tests of significance, labeled "Joint F-tests." These are F-tests of the null hypothesis that all coefficients for variables in a particular grouping jointly equal zero. For example, the joint F-test of electoral vulnerability tests the null that the effects of the incumbent's previous vote share, challenger experience in the last election, and the spending gap in the last election jointly equal zero. District demand characteristics always matter to the distribution

Table 2.1

Effects of Select Variables on the Distribution of Pork

Variables	Democratic Districts			Republican Districts		
	Distributive Spending	Contingent Liabilities	Defense Pork	Distributive Spending	Contingent Liabilities	Defense Pork
Polarization	0.253* (0.114)	0.515* (0.209)	5.603* (1.084)	−0.035 (0.119)	0.953* (0.140)	5.961* (1.258)
DW-NOMINATE	0.184 (0.112)	0.461* (0.129)	−0.578 (0.769)	0.147 (0.103)	−0.400* (0.112)	0.364 (0.758)
District liberalism	0.594* (0.178)	0.385 (0.294)	4.744* (1.588)	0.444* (0.204)	−0.080 (0.263)	−0.228 (2.061)
Joint F-tests						
Electoral vulnerability	0.55	1.85	2.31	0.72	0.41	0.85
Legislator characteristics	2.13*	14.29*	0.95	2.99*	6.89*	0.36
District characteristics	5.00*	7.56*	11.10*	4.43*	8.03*	8.29*
Model statistics						
Observations	1,980	1,969	1,971	1664	1665	1649
Model F	4.40*	19.47*	20.04*	4.58*	19.84*	24.36*
R^2	0.112	0.385	0.302	0.152	0.480	0.320

Source: Author's analysis of data from Adler (n.d.), Bonica (2013), Lewis et al. (2019), Nelson (n.d.), Poole (2015), Stewart and Woon (2017), U.S. Bureau of the Census (n.d., 2002, 2011a, 2011b), and U.S. Bureau of Fiscal Service (2019).
* $p < 0.05$ (two-tailed)

Note: Coefficients and robust standard errors, included in parentheses, are presented for polarization, DW-NOMINATE scores, and district liberalism. Results in the "Joint F-test" panel present F-tests of the null hypothesis that all coefficients for variables in a given category (e.g., legislator characteristics) equal zero. All models control for electoral vulnerability, characteristics of the member, and characteristics of the district, as described in the text. Contingent liability models include a control for the 111th Congress. Defense pork models include controls for the 110th and 111th congresses. All models, except for the changes in contingent liability awards, control for the log of spending on the relevant projects and programs from the previous congress. Full results are available from the author upon request.

of benefits. To be sure, different characteristics are relevant to different measures of pork. Legislators, however, are responsive to the makeup of their districts. In contrast to district characteristics, measures of electoral vulnerability seem not to affect the distribution of pork. The measures analyzed here use total spending and awards. Given that prior research has found a link between electoral vulnerability and the acquisition of new spending, these null results are not surprising. Legislator characteristics are predictive of distributive spending and contingent liabilities, but not of defense pork. The null results for defense pork are similar to the findings of a number of studies that report weak relationships between characteristics such as roll-call behavior or committee membership and defense appropriations (Goss 1972; Ray 1981a, 1981b; Thorpe 2014). Table 2.1 does not present the effects of lagged spending or the congress dummies. These had the expected effects. In the distributive spending and defense pork models, receiving a larger amount of spending in the previous congress tends to decrease the relative amount of spending in the current congress. Also as expected, there is a significant increase in defense pork for both parties in the 110th Congress and in contingent liabilities in the 111th Congress.

Figures 2.4 through 2.6 present the effects of polarization, legislator ideology, and district liberalism, respectively, on the three measures of the pork barrel. Most importantly from the perspective of my argument, polarization does affect the distribution of pork largely in the expected ways. As polarization increases, Democratic districts see increases in distributive spending and Republican districts see increases in contingent liability awards and defense pork. This suggests that polarization causes members of Congress to pursue pork that is ideologically consistent with their districts. Figure 2.4, however, also shows that as polarization increases, Democrats pursue more of all types of pork while Republicans appear more ideologically focused in their pork barreling. Specifically, a standard deviation in polarization, equal to about 0.2, leads to an increase of 5 percent in distributive spending relative to spending in the previous congress in Democratic districts. Contingent liabilities and defense pork increase 10 percent and 112 percent, respectively. In Republican districts, the increases in contingent liabilities and defense pork are 19 percent and 119 percent, respectively.

Unlike polarization, legislator ideology has little effect on the distribution of pork, as depicted in figure 2.5. Further, once partisanship is accounted for, where the effects of legislator ideology are statistically significant, they are inconsistent. Legislator ideology affects only the distribution of contingent liability awards. A standard deviation increase

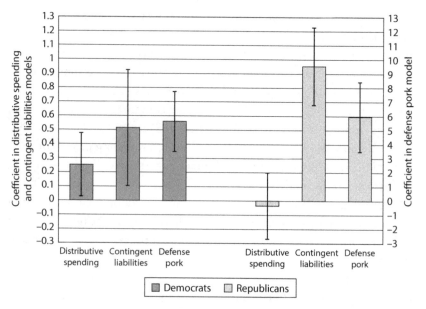

FIGURE 2.4 **Effects of polarization on the distribution of pork**
The first two solid bars in each set represent the coefficients for polarization in the distributive spending and contingent liability models and are scaled along the left axis. The third bar in each set represents the coefficient for polarization in the defense pork model. It is scaled along the right axis. Error bars represent 95 percent confidence intervals. *Source*: Author's analysis of data from Adler (n.d.), Bonica (2013a), Lewis et al. (2019), Nelson (n.d.), Poole (2015), Stewart and Woon (2017), U.S. Bureau of the Census (n.d., 2002, 2011a, 2011b), and U.S. Bureau of Fiscal Service (2019).

in DW-NOMINATE scores, equal to 0.44, increases relative contingent liability awards by 20 percent in Democratic districts and decreases them by 18 percent in Republican districts. As much of my discussion of polarization has already noted, party and ideology are linked, even more so in recent decades. Bickers and Stein (2000) find a partisan bias in support for distributive spending and contingent liabilities. They suggest that these partisan effects are based in ideological preferences. Given that Republicans are, on average, far more conservative than Democrats, the estimation of models on partisan subsamples is likely masking some of the effects of ideology. Though not depicted here, Republican districts do receive significantly more contingent liability awards than Democratic

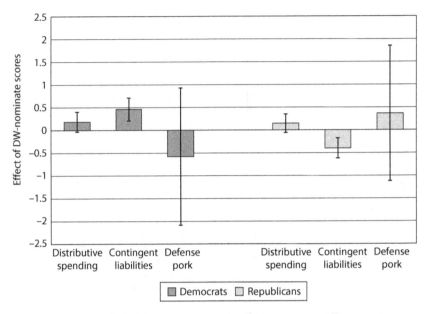

FIGURE 2.5 **Effects of legislator ideology on the distribution of pork**
Bars represent the coefficient of first dimension DW-NOMINATE scores on all three measures of pork. Error bars represent 95 percent confidence intervals. *Source*: Author's analysis of data from Adler (n.d.), Bonica (2013a), Lewis et al. (2019), Nelson (n.d.), Poole (2015), Stewart and Woon (2017), U.S. Bureau of the Census (n.d., 2002, 2011a, 2011b), and U.S. Bureau of Fiscal Service (2019).

districts, on average.[10] Lazarus and Reilly (2010) find that contingent lia-bility spending benefits Republicans in conservative districts, but not in liberal ones. Combining these observations, it can be argued that ideol-ogy is meaningful to the distribution of contingent liabilities in the pre-dicted ways. Owing to their generally conservative nature, Republicans pursue contingent liabilities. Similarly, there is an increased preference for contingent liabilities among conservative Democrats, who have inci-dentally all but disappeared from the House of Representatives.[11]

Completing the discussion of ideology, district liberalism has effects on the pork barrel that are mostly consistent with expectations. As shown in figure 2.6, district liberalism is relevant to the pursuit of distributive spend-ing by legislators in both parties. A standard deviation increase in district liberalism, 0.14, increases relative distributive spending by 8 percent in

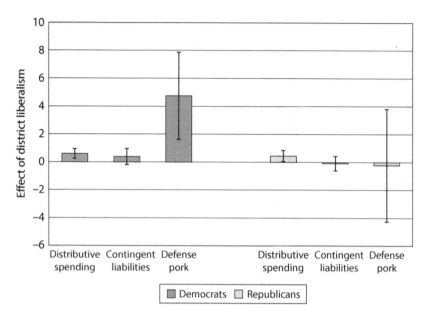

FIGURE 2.6 **Effects of district liberalism on the distribution of pork**
Bars represent the coefficient of district liberalism, measured as the district vote share of the Democratic candidate in the most recent presidential election, on all three measures of pork. Error bars represent 95 percent confidence intervals. *Source*: Author's analysis of data from Adler (n.d.), Bonica (2013a), Lewis et al. (2019), Nelson (n.d.), Poole (2015), Stewart and Woon (2017), U.S. Bureau of the Census (n.d., 2002, 2011a, 2011b), and U.S. Bureau of Fiscal Service (2019).

Democratic districts and 6 percent in Republican districts. The only other effect district liberalism has is on defense pork in Democratic districts. Contrary to the expectation that such spending would be preferred by conservative constituencies, increasing liberalism in Democratic districts increases defense pork; the increase is a sizable 66 percent for a standard deviation increase in the district vote share of Democratic presidential candidates.

Polarization, Ideology, and the Pork Barrel

I had two goals in writing this chapter. The first was to identify measures of the pork barrel that carry ideological meaning. While the literature makes persuasive cases for distributive spending and contingent liabilities, defense pork is more complex. As noted earlier, the remainder of this book uses measures of distributive spending and contingent liability, but not defense pork. Defense spending has important partisan and ideological features and is strongly supported by congressional Republicans. Defense pork, however, on the evidence presented here, in other research, and in empirical examinations I have conducted but not presented here, operates differently than the other, more ideologically grounded pork barrel measures. Similar to the pursuit of contingent liabilities, defense pork increases with polarization in Republican districts. On its face, this suggests an ideological character of defense pork and that Republicans believe defense pork will be preferred by their voters. The major problem with this conclusion is that the same is true of Democrats, for whom the effects of polarization are just as strong and positive. Unlike contingent liabilities, there is no evidence that Republicans receive more defense pork. In raw terms, Republican districts receive $17 million more in defense pork, on average, but using the natural log of spending produces a distribution that is skewed slightly toward Democratic districts. Neither difference is statistically significant.

Similarly, the direct connections to conservatism are nonexistent here. Legislator ideology is not predictive of relative defense pork. Furthermore, district liberalism correlates with increases in defense pork in Democratic districts. Whereas the pork barrel is generally considered to be part of the broader issue domain of government spending that overlays liberal/conservative thought, defense spending may be part of a related but separate domain in the minds of voters. Some of this is backed up by the arguments and findings in Thorpe (2014), including the importance of economic reliance on defense industries, support for defense spending (conditioned by reliance) among Democrats, and the decreasing effect of ideology (conservatism) on Republican support for defense expenditures over time. On the last point, at least within the Republican Party, support for defense spending may be less an ideological preference for types of spending and more a tenet of Republican (not necessarily conservative) orthodoxy. As a final examination of whether defense pork evinces ideologically consistent partisan effects as polarization increases, I estimated all of the models presented in chapters 5, 6,

3

An Electoral History of the Pork Barrel

IN HIS VETO MESSAGE TO CONGRESS regarding the Maysville Road bill, which would have allowed the federal government to purchase stock in the company created to build a road between Maysville and Lexington, Kentucky, President Andrew Jackson wrote the following:

> The constitutional power of the Federal Government to construct or promote works of internal improvement presents itself in two points of view—the first as bearing upon the sovereignty of the States within whose limits their execution is contemplated. . . . In the first view the question of power is an open one, and can be decided without the embarrassments attending the other, arising from the practice of the Government. Although frequently and strenuously attempted, the power to this extent has never been exercised by the Government in a single instance. It does not, in my opinion, possess it; and no bill, therefore, which admits it can receive my official sanction. (Jackson 1830)

The general argument presented in the first chapter of this book is that political polarization conditions the electoral effects of federal distributive spending. That discussion highlighted two potential directions for these conditioning effects. The view common to much of the literature on distributive benefits presents the collection of these benefits as almost apolitical. Although different groups may favor certain types of projects and programs as opposed to others, as a whole the pork barrel is part of incumbency advantage. Members of Congress secure funding for the programs favored by their constituents and reap the electoral benefits of these efforts. In this way, I contrasted credit claiming for this spending with position taking, which emphasizes stances and votes on the issues salient to the electorate. If the pork barrel is merely another form of casework (Cain, Ferejohn, and Fiorina 1987), its electoral effects should be consistently positive. If political polarization conditions the electoral effects of the pork barrel at all, one would expect pork to have its strongest effects during periods of low polarization. When polarization is high, it is expected that voters will pay greater attention to positions their representatives have taken than to the in-district benefits those representatives have been able to secure.

Despite the prevalence of this view, I argue that the pork barrel is an ideological issue. Far from being a collection of programs for which incumbents get to claim credit, federal particularistic spending is, and always has been, an issue on which the parties, and the ideological groupings associated with them, have differed. Jackson's veto message highlights this ideologically based reaction to federal spending—the pork barrel as part of the broader issues of federal power and influence. This chapter begins by discussing the historical development of the pork barrel as an ideological and partisan issue. It concludes with a long-term, aggregate analysis of House election outcomes and public-works spending. The results demonstrate that public-works spending carries electoral benefits for Democrats and electoral costs for Republicans, and that these relationships are strongest during periods of heightened polarization.

A Brief History of the Pork Barrel as an Ideological Issue

"Pork barrel" is a pejorative term for a collection of supposedly wasteful federally funded projects—wasteful in the sense that the benefits of these projects are geographically concentrated, meaning that taxpayers are forced to fund many projects from which they receive little or no direct benefit. Pork barreling is also a process, a means of creating and passing legislation. Decrying the growth of the pork barrel in the early twentieth century, Chester Maxey (1919) equated the pork barrel with the use of the omnibus bill as a means of appropriating money for river and harbor projects. Pork barreling in this sense is the process by which multiple projects are combined into one piece of legislation to vastly increase the prospects for each project. When these projects were voted on individually, many of them failed, presumably because of the highly concentrated nature of the benefits. While logrolling tended to increase the likelihood of funding projects, the individualized nature of river and harbor appropriations was much too slow to meet the demands of constituents, and by extension their representatives, for federal money. The omnibus was an effective solution to the collective-action problem of project funding and a driver of universalism in the distribution of benefits. Placing nearly everyone's project in the omnibus guaranteed a sizable majority coalition in support of the single bill, with support for "bad" projects buoyed by support for "good" projects, as the fortunes of both were inexorably tied together (Maxey 1919).

The idea of the federal pork barrel is as old as the republic itself, even if its meaning and composition have changed dramatically over nearly two-and-a-half centuries. In its purest ideological form, opinions on the use of federal funds are part of one's attitudes regarding the size, scope, and influence of the federal government. Alexander Hamilton arguably contributed more than any other politician of the early republic to polarization on this issue through his economic plan for the nation. To Hamilton, internal improvements, as such spending was called throughout the late-eighteenth and nineteenth centuries, would bring much needed development to the new nation, placing it on a stronger footing to compete with the long-established nations of Europe (Hostetler 2011; O'Hara 2008; Wood 2009).[1] Opposition to Hamilton's plan emphasized the strengthening of federal authority that would result from its provisions, to the detriment of state and local autonomy, and became the catalyst for organized opposition to the Federalist Party (Wood 2009). Thus, from the outset, federal spending was inseparable from federal power, and partisan/ideological divisions over such issues would only strengthen over the next several decades.

Although the Federalist Party would disappear not long after the birth of the republic, federal spending on public works would remain a hotly debated issue well into the nineteenth century. As the Era of Good Feelings came to a close, federal funding for internal improvements would appear as one of the central aspects of Henry Clay's "American System" and become an article of faith for the Whig Party (Heidler and Heidler 2010; Holt 1999). As strongly as Whigs favored federally sponsored projects, Democrats were just as firm in their resistance. Especially as slavery became the single issue in American national politics, the Democratic Party would forcefully reject any exertion or growth of federal influence, except when that influence was directed toward protecting and expanding the South's "peculiar institution" (Howe 2007).

The common ideological thread linking Hamilton's economic plan and Clay's American System is the use of federal largesse to increase the influence of the central government. For proponents of this positive government, the power and treasure of the federal government could be directed toward improving the infrastructure of the nation, thereby increasing commerce and the economic well-being of all of the states. Opponents, however, feared that expanding federal influence in one sphere would expand federal influence in all spheres. After the party of Jefferson and Madison split, the Jacksonian Democratic Party developed an almost reflexive resistance to any exertion of federal power, except when that power was used specifically to protect and promote slavery. As slavery becomes the defining issue of the republic during the Jacksonian era, all other issues reflective of federal power, including and especially federally funded internal improvements, become key points of disagreement between the major parties. In discussing river and harbor legislation, one of the largest sources of distributive spending until the middle of the twentieth century (Ferejohn 1974; Maxey 1919), Chester Maxey notes that, starting from 1829, "despite strenuous attempts in every session of congress, there was no omnibus waterway legislation of any moment except in the year 1852 until after the Civil War" (1919, 692).

From the inauguration of George Washington until the Civil War, federal distributive spending existed as an issue on which the major parties were polarized. In a remarkable study of nineteenth-century distributive spending, Gordon and Simpson (2018) found that modern explanations for the distribution of pork (e.g., universalism) fail to explain legislator support for and opposition to this spending. The best explanation is the legislator's partisan-ideological preferences. The pork barrel would change after Reconstruction, however, as the nation entered an era of unbridled industrial growth with a growing thirst for federal backing of all manner of projects (Cashman 1993). Once the federal government essentially gave up policing the South, the Democratic Party, especially given the need to rebuild the South to compete with northern industry, becomes more disposed to federal public-works spending. While the Republican Party had inherited a preference for such spending from its Whig predecessor, this desire grew even more as the West developed, and as private interests found myriad ways of influencing public policy (Cashman 1993; Gordon and Simpson 2018). Given its dominance in national politics during this era, it seems inevitable that the taint of corruption in these private/public partnerships should tar the Republican Party, leaving within the rank and file a subgroup of people as distrustful of federal influence in most matters as were antebellum Democrats. Despite the growth of progressive, anticorruption sentiment, the pork barrel would grow throughout the end of the nineteenth and into the twentieth century, encompassing a wide variety of programs and projects, including the aforementioned river and harbor spending, public buildings (especially post offices), and agricultural spending (Maxey 1919).

Modern ideological preferences regarding government spending generally, and distributive spending specifically, developed as the nation grappled with the Great Depression. In an interesting reversal from its antebellum history, the Democratic Party developed with an emphasis on positive government as the nation entered the New Deal era (Hartz 1955; Hoover et al. 2001; Skocpol 1983). This new liberalism embraced state action. At its heart, the New Deal sought to protect the liberty and economic well-being of citizens through government intervention, including the use of large amounts of government spending on public works and other programs distributive in nature. Modern conservatism, developing within the Republican Party, responded by pushing back against many types of government spending (Nisbet 1984;

Rossiter 1982). As New Deal liberalism concentrated on government intervention to regulate economic and social equality, modern conservatism emphasized a return to the status quo of limited government, especially in relation to the economy. Philosophically, conservatism, as the name suggests, is rooted in aspects of tradition and resistance to radical change (Rossiter 1982). Insofar as New Deal liberalism represented a radical change in the nature of the role of government, particularly in the use of government programs, modern conservatism would oppose this growth in government intervention (Nisbet 1984). In the second half of the twentieth century, it can be argued, the nature of federal spending, or at least what the mass public thinks about when prompted about government spending, changed. Government spending up through the beginning of the New Deal era was likely more closely entwined with distributive spending than it would be as the nation transitioned out of the 1930s. The New Deal, and especially the Great Society of the 1960s, vastly increased federal spending on social-welfare programs.[2] These changes occurred during a period that saw the beginning of the Cold War and significant growth in military spending. Over the past fifty years, this spending has encompassed more than 50 percent of the federal budget year after year (Executive Office of the President of the United States 2012); it is redistributive spending over which the parties have more visibly fought. Despite its decreased salience, reactions to the pork barrel are still rooted in the ideological fabric of the parties, giving them the potential to become divisive if conditions are right.

Data and Methods

Polarization has conditioned the effects of pork barrel spending on election outcomes since the end of Reconstruction. To illustrate this, I present analyses of aggregate House election results from 1878, just after the conclusion of the Reconstruction era, through 2012. As previously noted, one small drawback to much of the work on distributive benefits is that the empirical analyses are limited to the most recent era, with data sets typically starting in 1983, the first year for which FAADS data are available. The district- and individual-level analyses presented in the following chapters are similarly limited. This period, 1983 through today, is also one in which polarization, by most measures, is generally increasing. While there is sufficient variation in polarization during this period to give full discussion to its impact, the conclusions are necessarily limited to the role of polarization in this most recent era. The aggregate analyses presented in this chapter, though limited in other ways, demonstrate that polarization has conditioned the electoral impact of public spending at least since the end of Reconstruction.

Two models are presented, one for Democrats and one for Republicans. The dependent variables are the mean vote share in a given election year won by incumbents in each party. Party electoral fortunes have changed in systematic ways over the past nearly century-and-a-half. To account for these partisan realignments, the models are estimated with a random intercept, nesting congressional election years within four broad eras: post-Reconstruction and Progressive (1878–1932), the New Deal (1933–1960), the New Frontier (1961–1980), and the Reagan era realignment (1981–2012). The random intercept is used to capture the dominance of a particular political party in elections during each era—Republicans in the first and last and Democrats in the middle two—with eras reflecting research on partisan realignments and critical elections (Key 1955; Meffert, Norpoth, and Ruhil 2001; Nardulli 1995).[3]

Measuring the Pork Barrel and Polarization

A measure of pork barrel spending is difficult to find for such a long period. One measure that is available and relates to common conceptions of the "pork barrel" is public-works spending.[4] As Maxey (1919) notes, public works are the original pork barrel, starting with river and harbor legislation. Since the nineteenth century, public-works spending has come to encompass improvements of rivers and harbors, the construction and maintenance of roads and bridges, and the erecting of federal buildings, among many other projects. The data are drawn from two sources. From 1878 through 1939, these data are taken from annual publications of the

U.S. Department of the Treasury (n.d.).[5] From 1940 through 2012, data are taken from historical tables published by the Office of Management and Budget (Executive Office of the President of the United States 2015). The independent variable is the congress-difference in the natural logarithm of public-works spending, measured in constant 2009 dollars (e.g., the data point for the 2012 election is the natural log of spending for the 112th Congress minus the natural log of spending for the 111th Congress). The natural log of aggregate public-works spending since 1872 is presented in figure 3.1. The dollar-amount equivalents are listed along the right axis. For comparison purposes, figure 3.1 also plots the district averages for distributive spending and contingent liability awards over years for which those data are available. Even when measured in constant dollars, public-works spending, like other distributive spending, generally increased throughout the twentieth and twenty-first centuries. Congress to congress, however, there are certainly periods during which public-works spending stayed relatively flat or decreased—around major wars, for example.

As with the pork barrel, I am unable to use the measure of polarization in these analyses that is used in the rest of this work. The analyses in this chapter use a polarization scale derived from House DW-NOMINATE scores (McCarty, Poole, and Rosenthal 1997) and party votes. Specifically, the House polarization scale is a Likert scale combining standardized versions of the difference between the Democratic and Republican mean first-dimension DW-NOMINATE scores, the difference between mean second-dimension DW-NOMINATE scores, and the proportion of House roll calls that were 50–50 party votes.[6] Cronbach's α for the scale is 0.790. Figure 3.2 shows both the House polarization scale, calculated from 1876 through 2012, and the ANES polarization scale presented in chapter 2, calculated from 1964 through 2012. Both show polarization at a nadir in the 1960s, then climbing steadily until reaching the peaks of the last several years. The House polarization scale shows that polarization over the past thirty years has been at levels comparable to polarization in the post-Reconstruction era through the beginning of the twentieth century. Though there is not a perfect correspondence between them, the two measures correlate at a value of 0.744 over the period from 1964 through 2012.[7]

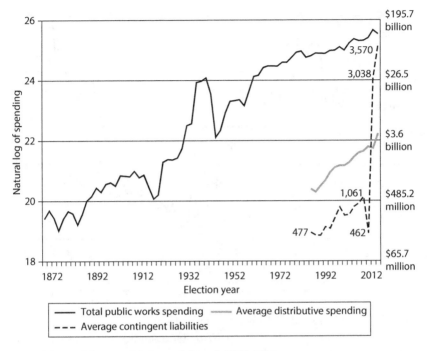

FIGURE 3.1 **Measures of the pork barrel, 1872–2012**

The lines for public-works and average distributive spending represent the two-year totals of the natural logarithm of constant 2009 dollars (e.g., the value for 2012 is the log of total spending in 2011 and 2012). Values of the natural log are placed on the left axis and the equivalent dollar amounts on the right axis. Because the trend in spending has been positive, especially in the public-works series, changes look more exaggerated earlier in the series, when dollar values were relatively small, and more muted later in the series, when dollar values were relatively large. Values for average contingent liability awards do not correspond to those presented on either axis. Instead, value labels are used at selected points. For example, in 1983 and 1984, the average was 477 total awards. The average gradually increased to 1,061 in the 2005–2006 period, dropped to 462 in the 2007–2008 period, spiked to 3,038 in the 2009–2010 period, and climbed to 3,570 in the 2011–2012 period. *Source*: Executive Office of the President of the United States (2015), U.S. Bureau of the Census (n.d.), U.S. Bureau of Fiscal Service (2019), and U.S. Department of the Treasury (n.d.).

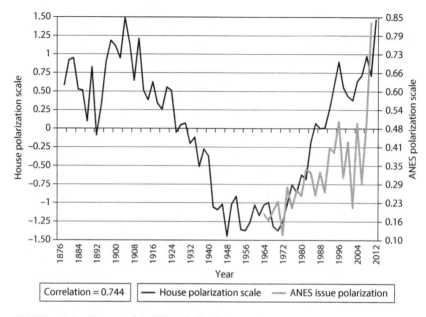

FIGURE 3.2 **House and ANES polarization scales**
As described in the text, the House polarization scale ($\alpha = 0.790$) varies by congress and is comprised of standardized versions of the differences between the mean Democratic and Republican DW-NOMINATE scores on the first and second dimensions, as well as the proportion of roll-call votes that were 50–50 party votes. The ANES polarization scale, which also varies biennially, is the mean difference between Democratic and Republican identifiers on a scale comprised of several issue attitudes. *Source*: Author's analysis of data from American National Election Studies (2007, 2011, 2015), Lewis et al. (2019), and Poole (2015).

Given the discussion of pork as an ideological issue, it is expected that public-works spending has an increasingly positive effect on Democratic vote share and an increasingly negative effect on Republican vote share as polarization increases. The models also include several control variables thought to influence aggregate party fortunes in congressional elections (Jacobson 1989; Tufte 1975). A dummy variable is included indicating Democratic presidents. The party of the president by itself is not expected to affect election outcomes; it is included because the next three variables discussed are reverse-coded when the president is Republican. The first of these is an indicator for midterm election years, which are expected to harm incumbents from the president's party. The second is the percent change in real gross domestic product (RGDP) for the year of the election, expected to benefit incumbents from the president's party.[8] The third is an indicator for wartime elections, including elections for which a major war was ongoing at any point during the election year.[9] The final two control variables are meant to capture changes in party fortunes from election to election. The first is the national popular vote share of the party's candidate in the most recent presidential election, which is expected to have a positive effect on the mean vote share of that party's incumbents. The second is an indicator for wave elections, defined as an election in which one party gains at least 10 percent of the seats in the House. The wave variable is coded 1 for Democratic waves and −1 for Republican waves.[10]

The Electoral Effects of Public-Works Spending

Table 3.1 presents the results for Democratic and Republican House incumbents. Note that despite the time-series nature of the data, neither model's residuals exhibit unit root behavior, as evidenced by the Dickey-Fuller tests. Looking first at the control variables, the mean vote share of Democratic incumbents is roughly 3.5 points lower during midterm elections when the president is a Democrat; it is 3.5 points higher when the president is Republican. The change in mean Republican incumbent vote share is nine-tenths of a point during midterm elections. Several variables affect only the mean vote share of Republican incumbents. First, a 1 percent increase in the annual percentage change in RGDP increases mean Republican vote share by two-tenths of a point when the president is a Republican, decreasing it by that amount when the president is a Democrat. Second, a one-point increase in the Republican presidential candidate's national popular vote share is expected to increase mean Republican House incumbent vote share by about 0.158. Third, the average vote share of Republican incumbents significantly and substantially changes during wave years, with mean vote swings of 4.5 points in wave elections. The final control variable, wartime elections, significantly affects mean Democratic vote share, but not mean Republican vote share. Mean Democratic incumbent vote share decreases almost

Table 3.1
Results for Mean House Incumbent Vote Share Models

Variable	Democrats		Republicans	
	Coefficient	Std. Err.	Coefficient	Std. Err.
Polarization	0.003	0.007	0.003	0.011
Public-works spending	0.028	0.025	−0.022*	0.005
x Polarization	0.026*	0.008	−0.018*	0.007
Democrat president	0.018*	0.008	0.002	0.008
Midterm	−0.035*	0.007	0.009*	0.003
% change in RGDP	0.001	0.001	−0.002*	0.000
Wartime election	−0.019*	0.005	−0.003	0.008
Presidential vote share	0.024	0.059	0.158*	0.018
Wave election	0.022	0.019	−0.045*	0.007
Intercept	0.635*	0.018	0.543*	0.016
Model statistics				
Observations	68		68	
Overall R^2	0.521		0.5181	
Dickey-Fuller test	−5.287 ($p < 0.001$)		−4.203 ($p < 0.001$)	
Hausman test (FE v. RE)	8.69 ($p = 0.466$)		1.13 ($p = 0.999$)	

Source: Author's analysis of data from Executive Office of the President of the United States (2015), Johnston and Williamson (2019), King (1995), Lewis et al. (2019), Poole (2015), U.S. Bureau of Economic Analysis (2018), and U.S. Department of the Treasury (n.d.).

* $p < 0.05$ (two-tailed)

Note: Standard errors are robust. Midterm elections, percent change in RGDP, and wartime elections, which are listed in italics, are reverse coded when the president is Republican. Both models include random intercepts for four broad eras of American politics: 1878–1932, 1933–1960, 1961–1980, and 1980–2012. The Dickey-Fuller test was conducted on the residuals of each model to test for unit root behavior. Neither of the residuals exhibits this. Lastly, a Hausman test was used to ascertain whether the random intercept by era was appropriate. The tests show no significant differences between the estimates of fixed-effects versus random-effects models.

two points during a major war when the commander in chief is a Democrat and increases by the same amount during Republican administrations. Given the wars included and the number of elections held during each war period, these effects are likely being driven by mounting public dissatisfaction with the party of the commander in chief during the two longest war periods: Vietnam and the War on Terror (Mueller 1973; Norpoth and Sidman 2007; Sidman and Norpoth 2012).

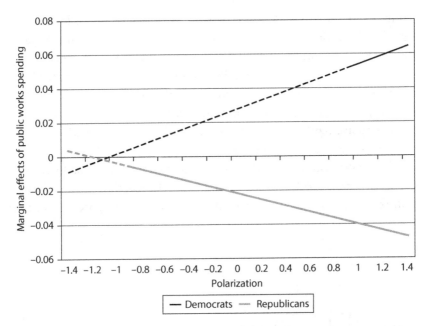

FIGURE 3.3 **Marginal effects of public-works spending on mean incumbent vote share**
The dashed portions of the curves identify where the marginal effects of public-works spending do not achieve statistical significance. *Source*: Author's analysis of data from Executive Office of the President of the United States (2015), Johnston and Williamson (2019), King (1995), Lewis et al. (2019), Poole (2015), U.S. Bureau of Economic Analysis (2018), and U.S. Department of the Treasury (n.d.).

Figure 3.3 presents the marginal effects of public-works spending across the range of polarization. For both parties, the results support the argument that pork barrel spending, at least in the form of public-works spending, is an ideological issue. As polarization increases, public-works spending has an increasingly positive effect on mean Democratic incumbent vote share. The effects, however, are not statistically significant until polarization, which ranges from roughly −1.5 to 1.5, reaches the higher portion of its range, starting at 0.9. Thus when polarization is high, increases in public-works spending benefit Democratic House incumbents. For Republicans, as polarization increases, the effects become increasingly negative. Public-works spending significantly affects mean Republican vote share starting at much lower levels of polarization (from a value of −0.9) than for Democrats, although at the lowest levels of polarization, public-works spending has no significant impact. Placing these results in perspective, the mean congress-difference in the natural log of public-works spending is roughly 0.1. At an elevated level of polarization—a value of 1, for example—this increase in public-works spending is expected to increase mean Democratic vote share by more than five-tenths of a point. Mean Republican vote share is expected to decrease by four-tenths of a point.

The results also suggest when in time each party more broadly felt the effects of public-works spending. Figure 3.4 depicts the House polarization scale across time, similar to the presentation in figure 3.2. In this

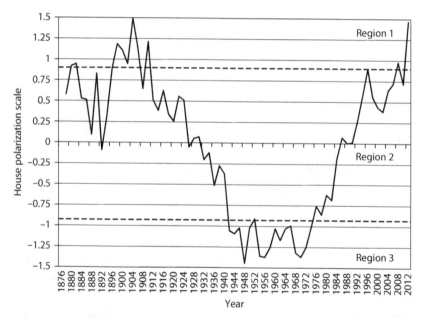

FIGURE 3.4 **Significance of public-works spending**
In region 1 of the graph, public-works spending is significant for both Democrats and Republicans. In region 2, public-works spending is significant only for Republicans. In region 3, public-works spending is significant for neither party. *Source:* Author's analysis of data from Executive Office of the President of the United States (2015), Johnston and Williamson (2019), King (1995), Lewis et al. (2019), Poole (2015), U.S. Bureau of Economic Analysis (2018), and U.S. Department of the Treasury (n.d.).

figure, the different regions identify where public-works spending is significant: for both parties in region 1, for Republicans only in region 2, and for neither party in region 3. For Republicans, public-works spending has significant negative effects for most of the period examined here, except for the period between the end of World War II and the end of the Vietnam War. For Democrats, the situation is largely the reverse. Public-works spending is not significant for most of the period examined here. It is significant, with a few exceptions, from 1878 through 1912 and from 1996 through 2012. Relating this to the historical discussion earlier in the chapter, one could surmise that the pork barrel is rarely salient enough to typical Democratic voters for the issue to affect their behavior. In the post-Reconstruction era, the Democratic Party, still adapting its antebellum positions to a changed nation, is rather ambivalent toward the pork barrel. Even Roosevelt's emphasis on positive government and the development of a new liberalism was rooted less in "spending" and more in addressing the needs of the various constituencies of the New Deal coalition (Stuckey 2015). It is not until polarization is high, and nearly every issue is a battleground for partisan conflict, that the pork barrel systematically and significantly affects the electoral fortunes of Democratic representatives.

Conclusion

Spending on public works represents the classic pork barrel project (e.g., the new post office, bridge maintenance) that constituents are assumed to favor regardless of their political predispositions. Building these projects means employment in the community, purchases from local suppliers, and a finished product from which local residents will benefit. Despite this, public-works spending, like the pork barrel broadly, is rooted in ideological conflict. The foregoing discussion has suggested a rationale for conservative opposition to public-works spending, which finds support in the empirical analysis. The results point to two conclusions relevant to the analyses in the remainder of this book.

First, and most importantly, polarization conditions the effects of the pork barrel in ideologically meaningful ways. The pork barrel was born with spending on public works (rivers and harbor legislation), and public works remained the primary type of pork barrel spending into the twentieth century. It is the type of spending scholars had in mind when explaining universalism in the distribution of benefits, and it is supposed to be at the core of credit claiming by incumbents. Yet Republicans have generally suffered electorally as spending on public works has grown, except during periods of very low polarization that included two major wars and the massive growth of the welfare state. Since the post-Reconstruction era, a faction within the Republican Party has been suspicious of government power. This desire for a return to limited government would become the basis of the modern conservative ideology that found its home in the Republican Party during the New Deal era. Democrats, on the other hand, have benefited from public-works spending. With slavery gone as an issue, a pressing need to rebuild Democratic strongholds in the South, and the Republican Party agreeing to abandon Reconstruction in 1877, the Democratic Party began to embrace the positive power of government. By 1933, the use of federal funds to protect and advance society became an important part of the liberal Democratic ideology. The pork barrel is not always relevant to elections. As the results demonstrate, polarization must be sufficiently high for the pork barrel to affect the electoral fortunes of incumbents.

The second conclusion relevant to this work is that public-works spending is meaningful for Republicans across a far larger range of polarization than it is for Democrats. The results suggest that typical Republican constituencies are more tuned to this type of government spending than are typical Democratic constituencies. It is this keener awareness of spending that is likely the reason for the more complex relationships between the pork barrel and elections that exist for Republicans. Both of these conclusions have roots in the development of liberalism and conservatism, which is explored at the individual level in the next chapter.

4

Attitudes, Voting, and the Pork Barrel

THE STORY OF THE PORK BARREL in American politics is not just a story of individual attitudes, but the opinions and behavior of the mass public do play a crucial part. Incumbents, challengers, and campaign donors all respond to an electoral context in which voters decide the outcome—voters who can be moved or persuaded under the right conditions. The previous chapter considered ideological reactions to the pork barrel from an aggregate, partisan perspective; this chapter explores the individual-level foundations for that electoral context. In the introductory chapter, I argued that the pork barrel is never a salient issue in its own right but that at high levels of polarization, there exist systematic links between the pork barrel and attitudes on government spending. I further argue that the pork barrel affects behavior, conditioned by the ideological dispositions that correlate with those attitudes. The following pages present the empirical evidence supporting these arguments.

The historical discussion in the previous chapter presents the backdrop against which ideological dispositions regarding the pork barrel develop. Elites in each party are largely responsible for cultivating support for or opposition to government spending. As they set forth the rationale for their positions, partisans in the mass public respond in kind (Hetherington 2001; Zaller 1992). While overall government spending is as an issue over which the parties and their ideological supporters perennially divide, the pork barrel rarely rises to that level of salience. Despite what can seem like the universal appeal of the pork barrel, it is a part of government spending and is more closely related to attitudes on spending as polarization increases. Foreshadowing the results, there are significant relationships between the pork barrel and attitudes and between the pork barrel and voting behavior. As polarization increases, distributive spending leads to increasing support for incumbents among liberals and decreasing support among conservatives. The results support an ideology-based explanation for the partisan results observed at aggregated levels of analysis.

Ideology in the American Context

From some of the earliest empirical studies of voting, exemplified by *The American Voter* (Campbell et al. 1960), we have known that preferences can have a strong effect on voting behavior, even if the public sometimes fails to express ideologically consistent opinions (Converse 1964). The notion that individuals could be ideologically opposed to all distributive spending runs counter to the prevailing assumption that rational individuals prefer more benefits to fewer benefits. This rationale, however, gives little guidance when trying to explain the empirical result that Republicans can suffer electorally when they overspend on their districts. The discussion of the pork barrel throughout American history has highlighted the ideological disagreements over this form of government spending. These disagreements are most readily observed at the elite level, where ideological views of the proper role of government shape partisan conflict among officeholders. Whether individuals in the mass public come to an ideological disposition on their own or take cues from elites, these differing opinions over distributive benefits, when salient, can shape mass behavior as well.

Despite "growing up" in the same traditions and history, there are strong differences in the meanings of "conservative" and "liberal" in America. Throughout the history of this country, identification along ideological lines has been influenced by the competing values underlying American tradition (McClosky 1958; McClosky and Zaller 1984).

The work on core beliefs and values identifies three major orientations: democracy, capitalism/individualism, and egalitarianism. As the ideas of liberalism and conservatism have developed, especially since the 1930s, they have seemed to become more organized around one of these values. Liberalism and "liberal" attitudes place more emphasis on egalitarianism—equality both in opportunity and outcomes—whereas conservatism has organized itself more around the value of capitalism (Conover and Feldman 1981; Feldman 1988; McClosky and Zaller 1984). Organization around values relates to the historical development of these ideologies, discussed in the previous chapter. To briefly recount that discussion, liberalism developed in its modern form with the New Deal in the 1930s, although it has undergone a variety of changes since the political unrest of the 1960s and 1970s (Dionne 1992). Modern conservatism developed largely in response to the policies of the New Deal. With liberalism and conservatism emphasizing different core values, we expect liberals and conservatives to display different preferences for all manner of political outcomes.

Their reactions to political information, however, may not oppose one another equally. Liberals, given the focus on equality, may be more inclined to respond to policies meant to create equal economic and social ends, while conservatives, given an ideological development in reaction to the New Deal, may be more interested in the economic outputs of government. Conover and Feldman (1981) show that individuals base their evaluations of liberals and conservatives—and by extension base their self-placement—on responses to different stimuli. Simply, what makes people want to be liberal does not necessarily make them oppose conservatism. Opposing, but unequal, reactions have been observed in preferences for spending in many issue domains (Rudolph and Evans 2005), and specifically on the social-welfare state (Feldman and Steenbergen 2001; Feldman and Zaller 1992; Skitka and Tetlock 1993).[1] One could posit a similar dynamic for the pork barrel. As previously described, overall distributive spending, especially direct payment and grant programs, bear some relation to the egalitarianism that drives liberal identification and preferences. While "egalitarian" takes on a different connotation for social welfare, given the targeting of benefits to more vulnerable members of society, distributive spending represents government's equalizing of outcomes. On the other hand, contingent liabilities are the distributive embodiment of individualism. These programs promote private behavior, ideally giving private entities the ability to succeed on their own terms. This distinction is of the utmost importance for reactions to the pork barrel because of the differing nature of these programs.

The discussion of values is meant to highlight that "ideology" is not necessarily a unidimensional construct and that liberals and conservatives may need to be considered differently, not just as different ends of the same continuum. While values undoubtedly play a less obvious role in judgments regarding the pork barrel, they are important in that they contribute to general ideological stances that in turn guide individuals toward preferences for the pork barrel. The differing orientations of liberals and conservatives may also extend beyond preferences to the overall salience of the pork barrel when attitudes are translated into behavior. Given the development of a redistributive, social-welfare focus in liberal policy since the New Deal era, it may be that liberals and conservatives tally information about distributive spending differently. Specifically, sharper reactions to the pork barrel might be found among conservatives, who are more sensitive to changes in overall government spending. This supposition is buttressed by recent examinations of polarization that find Republican voters have become more extreme than Democratic voters (Abramowitz 2015; Bonica et al. 2015). Not all conservatives, however, may be created equally in this regard. Ellis and Stimson (2012) provide ample discussion of what they call "conflicted conservatives." Such individuals tend to vote Republican, especially in presidential elections, express conservative identities, but hold liberal positions especially on economic issues. Ellis and Stimson do not provide much analysis of this operational-symbolic conflict among different levels of ideological intensity, but they note that "the ability to align a conservative self-identification with a conservative operational worldview correctly is related, but only loosely, to the strength of that identification" (2012, 103). From this, one could hypothesize that greater consistency, and therefore stronger effects of the pork barrel, would be found among more extreme ideological identifiers.

Symbolic-operational consistency could also result from, or at least correlate with, increasing polarization. Ellis and Stimson, examining decades' worth of survey data, find that liberals generally express consistency between their self-identification and issue positions while this consistency is less frequent among conservatives. For more than a decade, however, a number of scholars have explored this polarized environment, and many have noted the emergence of a phenomenon most commonly referred to as sorting. The main characteristic of sorting in the mass public is a closer alignment of political identification, primarily partisan, with issue positions. Different from mass polarization, in which the entire public becomes ideologically divergent, sorting is a polarizing of attitudes within the partisan public—more Democrats becoming liberal and more Republicans becoming conservative, regardless of changes, if any, among Independents (Levendusky 2009). Studies have noted a growing consistency between party and ideological identification (Abramowitz and Saunders 2008; Levendusky 2009), between party identification and issue positions (Abramowitz and Saunders 2008; Garner and Palmer 2011), and among positions across a range of issues (Abramowitz and Saunders 2008; Garner and Palmer 2011). Sorting, given its emphasis on partisans in the mass public, is a middle ground between those who argue for increasing mass polarization and those who argue that the mass public has not polarized, exemplified by Fiorina, Abrams, and Pope (2006). The most common explanation for sorting is that elites polarize and the partisan public adopts these clarified party positions (Hetherington 2001; Levendusky 2009). The media may also play a role in mass partisan polarization (Levendusky 2013), although preexisting ideological consistency across issues might be a prerequisite for individuals to respond to elite polarization (Carmines, Ensley, and Wagner 2012). Among other things, mass partisan polarization has been responsible for increasing public activism (Abramowitz and Saunders 2008; Mason 2015, 2018) and increasing partisan-directed anger (Iyengar and Westwood 2015; Mason 2015, 2018; Wolf, Strachan, and Shea 2012).

Just as polarization and sorting have evinced increasing partisan-ideological consistency generally, I expect to see increasing consistency between partisan and ideological identification and reactions to the pork barrel. As elites polarize, they express more consistent views on issues, including government spending. This consistency is passed down to the partisan public, making Republicans and conservatives in general more consistently opposed to, and Democrats and liberals more consistently in favor of, government spending. I further argue that this increased consistency during periods of high polarization makes information about the pork barrel more relevant to mass attitudes and behavior. The next section discusses the role of information in attitude formation, and the rest of the chapter tests my assertions regarding the effects of polarization and the pork barrel on attitudes and voting.

Information on the Pork Barrel

One issue with which work on distributive benefits has always grappled is linking the distributive activity of legislators to constituent knowledge of these activities. Individuals tend to exhibit very low levels of knowledge about even the most basic information regarding their representation in Congress. Yet numerous works have found that voters use information to update their evaluations of candidates, even if they cannot later recall the specific information (Lodge, McGraw, and Stroh 1989; Lodge, Steenbergen, and Brau 1995); the same has also been found for credit claiming in a distributive politics context (Grimmer, Messing, and Westwood 2012). There has also been a great deal of work linking information to candidate evaluations and voting behavior in a variety of contexts. For example, there is work looking at campaigns generally (Druckman 2004), campaign advertising specifically (Gerber et al. 2011; Goldstein and Freedman 2000), and the role of the media (Hetherington 1996). The point is that individuals can receive information, have that information change their attitudes and behavior, and then forget the specifics, with only the change in affect remaining.

A major impediment to addressing the question of voter knowledge empirically is that these items rarely appear in surveys and polls. Despite this lack of data, one could assume that individuals are at least exposed to information about this type of government spending because information on distributive politics comes from a variety of sources. The media report on pork barrel spending, although the information is likely to be negative. Media reports on distributive spending often use terms like "pork barrel" and "earmarks," which connote wasteful spending by the government. Information can also be obtained from interest groups. Many groups lobby for distributive programs and disseminate information on incumbent activities, especially during campaigns. There are also groups that promote fiscal responsibility and supply information (mostly negative) about specific representatives and senators (e.g., Citizens Against Government Waste and the National Taxpayers Union). The introductory chapter included a quote from a local opinion leader, yet another source of information about the distributive activities of representatives. Arguably, however, the best source of information regarding the incumbent's distributive activities is likely to be the incumbent herself. Through campaign advertising, mass mailings, or other communication with constituents, incumbents are usually more than willing to claim credit for what they believe to be district service.

Despite the ideological foundations of attitudes regarding the pork barrel, it may be that ideology is itself unnecessary if the primary source of information is through credit claiming. Given the monetary advantage most incumbents have, it is unlikely that challengers and their supporters will be able to effectively counter credit claiming by the incumbent. This uniformity in messaging, which would be pro-incumbent, should lead all voters who receive the message to evaluate the incumbent more favorably and increase the probability that an individual will vote for the incumbent (Stein and Bickers 1994a; Zaller 1992). Is this really true of information on government spending generally, or the pork barrel specifically? It may not be. Some empirical research has demonstrated that conservatives express opposition to spending *regardless of how the issue of spending is framed* (Jacoby 2000). In their discussion of framing, Ellis and Stimson note that proponents of liberal policies tend to avoid the government spending frame because it is more "controversial" (2012, 158). Relating this to credit claiming, even if incumbents present spending on distributive benefits in a positive manner, they risk having their conservative constituents look past the benefits and see only the spending.

The Pork Barrel and Attitudes on
Government Spending

One of the main assumptions underlying my argument is that the issues of the pork barrel and government spending are linked and the link strengthens as polarization increases. One major problem with assessing this assumption is that we lack good (or really any) measures of mass attitudes regarding the pork barrel specifically. A related issue is that items on government spending in most surveys either specify a type of spending that is not broadly distributive (e.g., social-welfare spending, which is redistributive, or defense spending, which is too specific) or leave the concept of government spending so broad as to possibly encompass any number of related issues. The following subsections present two analyses using data from the cumulative data file of the American National Election Studies (ANES). While the results do not provide iron-clad evidence, given the issues in finding measures of attitudes specific to distributive spending, they do identify both the link between pork and spending attitudes and the role that polarization plays in strengthening this relationship.

Government Spending as the
Most Important Problem

Even though survey items referencing government spending tend to keep that concept broad, the ANES does provide codes that are more specific for the item regarding the most important problem facing the country.[2] For the full data set, however, responses that reference government spending not related to defense, foreign affairs, or social welfare are coded together with responses referencing economic, business, and consumer concerns. Data on the specific reference (government spending not related to defense, foreign affairs, or social welfare), which I will refer to simply as "government spending," are limited to the years 1986 through 2000. Including the measure of polarization is not feasible because polarization was relatively low during most of this period. I can, however, examine whether there is a more general link between the pork barrel and considering government spending to be the most important problem.

To be frank, government spending is rarely the most important problem, both in an aggregate sense and an individual one. In the ANES, it is lumped together with more general economic concerns. In exit polls, it is not specified within the broad groupings of issues from which respondents can choose their answer. In the eight elections for which the specific data exist, 7.6 percent of respondents volunteered government spending as a response to the most-important-problem question. The likely marginal impact of government-spending-as-problem on other attitudes and behavior, however, does not diminish the importance of understanding the relationship, if any, between these attitudes and the pork barrel. Reponses to the most-important-problem question are dichotomized so that the response of government spending is coded 1 and all other valid responses are coded 0. The likelihood of stating that government spending is the most important problem is estimated with a probit model using the appropriate survey weights and adjusting the standard errors for clustering by election year.

The main independent variables are two of the measures of the pork barrel described in chapter 2: the congress-difference in logged distributive spending and the congress-difference in logged contingent liability awards. I control for the four campaign-related variables that are individually analyzed in chapters 5 and 6: whether the incumbent runs in a contested primary, whether the incumbent runs against an experienced challenger in the general election, the natural logarithm of challenger spending, and the natural logarithm of incumbent spending. I expect the first three variables to increase the likelihood of government spending's being mentioned as the most important problem. Generally, if government spending were going to register as a problem, the issue would probably be raised by those challenging the incumbent. Thus, primary challengers, experienced general-election challengers, and challengers spending more money could all raise the profile of government spending as an issue. Incumbent spending should have the opposite effect as the incumbent's campaign counters these critiques.[3]

I also control for several demographic and political characteristics of the respondents. Dummy variables are included for gender (female is

coded as 1) and race (black is coded as 1). The three-category party identification scale is used here, with Independent as the excluded category.
Ideological identification is measured as a five-category variable including codes for extremely liberal (excluded), liberal, moderate, conservative,
and extremely conservative.[4] Income percentile includes five categories:
0 through 16th percentile (excluded), 17th through 33rd, 34th through
67th, 68th through 95th, and 96th and above. Education level is included
as a four-category variable, with high school, some college, and college or
greater as variables in the model and grade school or less as the excluded
category. Lastly, I include national economic retrospections, coded as −1
(the economy has worsened over the past year), 0 (the economy has stayed
the same), or 1 (the economy has improved). It is generally expected that
characteristics more associated with reliance on government will lead to a
decreased likelihood of viewing government spending as the most important problem. Therefore, women and blacks are expected to be less likely
to give the government spending response. Conversely, increasing income
percentile, education level, and conservatism are expected to increase the
likelihood of saying government spending is the most important problem.
This likelihood is expected to decrease for Democrats and increase for
Republicans, given the general preferences for and against spending in
each party. Lastly, a more favorable evaluation of the economy should
decrease the likelihood of mentioning government spending as the most
important problem, whereas government spending should be a more
salient problem during times of economic decline.

Most-Important-Problem Results

Results of the probit model are presented in table 4.1. As expected,
Republican identification, greater conservatism, and higher education
level all increase the likelihood of naming government spending as the
most important problem. Being female or black, as well as more positive
evaluations of the economy, decrease the likelihood of singling out government spending. The final individual-level variable, income percentile,
generally has a positive association with viewing government spending
as the most important problem, but the effects are concentrated among

Table 4.1

Government Spending as the Most Important Problem

Variable	Coefficient	Std. Err.
Distributive spending	0.168*	0.065
Contingent liability awards	−0.057	0.057
Contested primary	−0.021	0.082
Experienced challenger	−0.085	0.101
ln(Challenger spending)	0.012*	0.006
ln(Incumbent spending)	−0.149*	0.057
Female	−0.288*	0.060
Black	−0.559*	0.128
Democrat	−0.039	0.038
Republican	0.115*	0.036
Ideology (Extremely liberal excluded)		
Liberal	0.170	0.180
Moderate	0.372*	0.163
Conservative	0.462*	0.151
Extremely conservative	0.371*	0.160
Income percentile (0–16th excluded)		
17th–33rd	0.144	0.110
34th–67th	0.193*	0.064
68th–95th	0.249*	0.118
96th–100th	0.090	0.130
Education level (Grade school excluded)		
High school	0.110	0.105
Some college	0.207*	0.081
College or greater	0.332*	0.087
Economic retrospections	−0.082†	0.047
Intercept	0.177	0.945
Model statistics		
Observations	5,681	
Log pseudolikelihood	−2,193.288	
LR χ^2 (6)	226.665*	
Percent correctly predicted	85.6%	

Source: Author's analysis of data from American National Election Studies (2015), Bonica (2013), U.S. Bureau of the Census (n.d.), and U.S. Bureau of Fiscal Service (2019).

*p < 0.05 (two-tailed)

†p < 0.05 (one-tailed, directional hypothesis expected)

Note: The model is estimated via probit. The dependent variable is coded 1 if the respondent selected government spending, as defined in the text, as the most important problem facing the nation, 0 if another issue was selected. Standard errors are adjusted for clustering by election year.

those in the 34th through 95th percentiles, in comparison to the poorest individuals and to those in the top 5 percent. Turning to campaign characteristics, both of the spending variables affect views of government spending as expected, with challenger spending increasing and incumbent spending decreasing the propensity to view government spending as the most important problem. Neither running in a contested primary nor against an experienced general-election challenger, however, significantly affects the government spending attitude examined here, after controlling for campaign spending. Most importantly, the pork barrel is positively related to viewing government spending as the most important problem. Specifically, increasing distributive spending increases the probability of government spending's being identified as the most important problem. Contingent liabilities, however, have no significant direct effects. As noted in the introductory chapter, contingent liabilities are markedly different from other forms of distributive spending and, as such, may not evince the same effects on government spending attitudes as total distributive spending.

Figure 4.1 graphically displays the effects of distributive spending on the predicted probability that government spending will be identified as the most important problem facing the nation. Predicted probabilities are calculated across the range of distributive spending merged into the ANES data, holding all other variables at mean or median values for continuous and categorical variables, respectively. Those values are 0.069 for the congress-difference in logged contingent liability awards, 9.746 for the log of challenger spending, and 13.277 for the log of incumbent spending, assuming an incumbent who ran in an uncontested primary and against a political amateur in the general election. Respondents are assumed to be male and white, identify as Independent and moderate, have income in the 34th through 67th percentile range, have high school as their highest level of educational attainment, and believe the economy has worsened over the past year. The figure simply shows what the direct effects suggest: as distributive spending increases, so does the predicted probability of government spending's being identified as the most important problem. Across the entire range of distributive spending, this probability increases from 0.065 to 0.4, a substantial increase of 0.335. Nearly all of the observations for distributive spending, however, fall in the

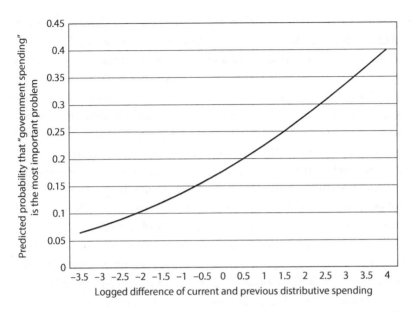

FIGURE 4.1 **The effect of distributive spending on "most-important-problem" responses**
The predicted probability of stating that government spending is the most important problem facing the nation is calculated across the full range of distributive spending for the ANES data. All other continuous and categorical variables are held at their mean or median values, respectively. *Source*: Author's analysis of data from American National Election Studies (2015), Bonica (2013a), U.S. Bureau of the Census (n.d.), and U.S. Bureau of Fiscal Service (2019).

−1 to 1 range. Even within this truncated range, the increase in predicted probability is 0.113. Overall, the results point to a solid link between increases in in-district pork barrel spending and the salience of government spending attitudes.

Spending and Services Attitudes

Despite the evidence that increasing distributive spending leads to an increased likelihood of singling out government spending as the most important problem facing the nation, there remains the question of whether increasing polarization strengthens the link between pork barrel spending and attitudes on government spending. To this end, I offer another analysis of ANES data, this time using a modification of the seven-point spending-services scale as the dependent variable.[5] The scale is recoded so that values of 1, 2, or 3, suggesting a preference for less spending and fewer services, are coded 1 and values of 4 through 7, suggesting preferences for the same level or more spending and services, are coded 0. As with the most-important-problem analysis, data here are not available for the full time frame. The analysis includes each presidential election year from 1992 through 2012, plus 1994. Unlike the previous analysis, the period for which these data are available includes greater variation in polarization, making for meaningful interpretations of the effects of the pork-polarization interactions, effects that will be further conditioned by the ideological self-identification of the respondent. Thus, the main independent variables are both measures of the pork barrel (the congress-difference of logged distributive spending and logged contingent liability awards), polarization, ideological self-identification coded as a five-point scale, and the interactions between pork, polarization, and ideology. The model is estimated using probit with the appropriate survey weights, adjusting the standard errors for clustering by election year. The model includes the following individual-level control variables from the most important problem analysis: gender (1=female), race (1=black), party identification (dummy variables for Democrat and Republican), income percentile (five categories), and education level (four categories). Additionally, I control for preferences for social-welfare spending.[6] The spending-services item is not specific regarding which "services" the respondent is to consider. Including preferences for social-welfare spending is a way to control for preferring greater overall spending because of preferences for greater spending in this more specific, nondistributive domain.

Explaining Preferences for Less Spending

Model results are presented in table 4.2. As with the most-important-problem analysis, all of the control variables have their expected effects on spending preferences. Women, blacks, Democrats, and those with preferences for increased welfare spending are all less likely to prefer

Table 4.2
Explaining Preferences for Less Spending

Variable	Coefficient	Std. Err.
Ideology (Extremely liberal excluded)		
Liberal	−0.187	0.361
x Polarization	0.967[†]	0.537
x Distributive spending	1.559*	0.624
x Polarization x DS	−2.911*	0.896
x Contingent liabilities	−2.592*	0.679
x Polarization x CL	4.755*	1.063
Moderate	−0.149	0.700
x Polarization	1.587	1.091
x Distributive spending	1.334*	0.233
x Polarization x DS	−2.357*	0.352
x Contingent liabilities	−2.188*	0.791
x Polarization x CL	3.917*	1.277
Conservative	0.143	0.836
x Polarization	1.939	1.310
x Distributive spending	0.884*	0.303
x Polarization x DS	−1.589*	0.440
x Contingent liabilities	−2.470*	0.547
x Polarization x CL	4.573*	0.823
Extremely conservative	0.586	0.741
x Polarization	1.165	1.126
x Distributive spending	1.206*	0.348
x Polarization x DS	−1.962*	0.483
x Contingent liabilities	−2.475*	1.095
x Polarization x CL	4.737*	1.870
Polarization	−0.602	0.869
Distributive spending	−0.983*	0.251
x Polarization	1.807*	0.378
Contingent liabilities	2.229*	0.717
x Polarization	−4.029*	1.126
Female	−0.200[†]	0.025
Black	−0.338[†]	0.071
Democrat	−0.359[†]	0.068
Republican	0.344[†]	0.034

(*continued*)

Table 4.2 (*Continued*)

Variable	Coefficient	Std. Err.
Income percentile (0–16th excluded)		
17th–33rd	−0.017	0.052
34th–67th	0.103*	0.044
68th–95th	0.132*	0.039
96th–100th	0.133†	0.080
Education (Grade school excluded)		
High school	−0.092	0.096
Some college	−0.001	0.102
College or greater	0.144	0.114
Welfare spending	−0.555*	0.065
Intercept	−0.945	0.506
Model statistics		
Observations	7,191	
Log Pseudolikelihood	−4,988.039	
LR χ^2 (5)	2,930.138*	
% Correctly predicted	75.8%	

Source: Author's analysis of data from American National Election Studies (2015), U.S. Bureau of the Census (n.d.), and U.S. Bureau of Fiscal Service (2019).

* p < 0.05 (two-tailed)

† p < 0.05 (one-tailed, directional hypothesis expected)

Note: The model is estimated via probit. The dependent variable is coded 1 if the respondent placed her or himself on the side of the seven-point scale favoring less spending and fewer services, 0 otherwise. Standard errors are adjusted for clustering by election year.

decreasing spending. The likelihood of preferring less spending and fewer services increases for Republicans and generally with income. Education level has no significant effects on spending preferences here. Most of the interactive effects between ideology, polarization, and the pork barrel are significant. To make sense of these effects, the discussion now turns to the marginal effects of the pork barrel measures under different conditions. Looking first at distributive spending, this measure of pork is almost always significant for extreme liberal identifiers and for moderate identifiers; that is, statistical significance is achieved across the range of polarization. Interestingly, when we look not across ideological identification, but across polarization, a more meaningful pattern develops. Beyond extreme liberals and moderates, distributive spending significantly affects spending preferences only at higher levels of polarization. The pattern is close to what is expected for each ideological identity. When polarization is high, increasing distributive spending decreases the likelihood of preferring less spending for liberals and moderates. To be clearer, during high polarization, increasing distributive spending leads liberals and moderates to want to keep government spending at the same level or increase it. For conservatives and extreme conservatives, the effect is the opposite: more pork leads to preferences for less spending. Oddly, the same effect is found for extreme liberals during high polarization. One could surmise that this might have to do with the type of spending. That is, in a high pork district, during high polarization, extreme liberals are equating distributive programs and projects with the "services" prompt in the question, instead of other types of government services for which they have stronger preferences. A quick look at the extreme liberals in the estimation sample shows that those preferring *less spending* and *fewer services* also favor *increased spending* on the poor (52.4 percent), child care (71 percent), AIDS research (68.4 percent), public schools (67.6 percent), financial aid for college students (76.5 percent), and the homeless (87.5 percent). Either these individuals are wildly inconsistent between their general and specific attitudes or, what I believe is more likely the case, they are counting as "services" projects and programs very different from the more typical social-welfare programs—projects and programs that are more reflective of the negative connotations of the "pork barrel." Figure 4.2 illustrates the effects of distributive spending on the probability of preferring less spending when polarization is assumed to be at a high level (equal to 0.8), which is where the marginal effects of distributive spending are significant for all ideological identities.

Despite the multitude of asterisks in table 4.2, contingent liability awards are not as significantly linked to spending preferences as they appear. In calculating the conditional significance of these marginal effects, one finds that the effects for moderates, conservatives, and extreme conservatives are essentially null across the range of polarization. The story is likely the same as what was assumed in the most-important-problem

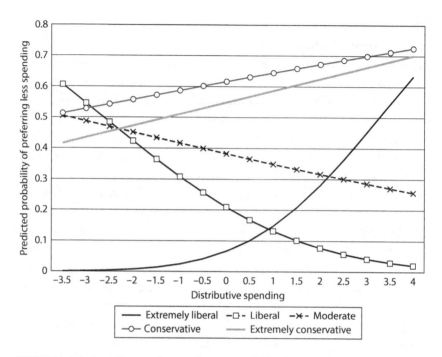

FIGURE 4.2 **Spending-services preferences and distributive spending during high polarization**

Note: Each curve represents the predicted probability of preferring less government spending (values of 1, 2, or 3 in the services-spending scale variable, *vcf0839*) for each of five categories of ideological identification across the range of the logged congress-difference in distributive spending. Control variables are held at the following: male, nonblack, Independent, income in the 34th through 67th percentile, high school graduate, and a preference for no change to federal welfare spending. *Source*: Author's analysis of data from American National Election Studies (2015), U.S. Bureau of the Census (n.d.), and U.S. Bureau of Fiscal Service (2019).

analysis. Contingent liabilities, representing a different type of spending, simply are not linked to the spending attitudes of these individuals. They are, however, linked, in opposing ways, to the attitudes of liberals and extreme liberals across the range of polarization. For liberals, the effect of contingent liability awards is an increasing function of polarization. At low levels of polarization, an increase in awards increases the likelihood of preferring constant or increasing levels of spending.

As polarization increases, this effect reverses, so that increasing awards leads to a greater probability of preferring less spending. For extreme liberals, it is the opposite. When polarization is low, increasing awards increases preferences for less spending. As polarization increases, the effect turns negative, with more awards spurring a desire for more (or constant) spending. As with distributive spending, I can only assume that the intensity of the ideological identification affects the way individuals process information about these programs. The extreme liberal sees more contingent liability awards and, tending to prefer other types of spending, wants more spending. The liberal sees more awards and wants that spending to stop.

Taken together, the results of the most-important-problem and spending-services analyses provide evidence of a major assumption underlying this theory: that the pork barrel and general spending attitudes are more systematically linked as polarization increases. Increasing pork, specifically distributive spending, increases the likelihood of seeing government spending as a problem. Furthermore, at high levels of polarization, increasing distributive spending generally pushes attitudes on spending and services in directions that are more consistent with the ideological self-identification of respondents, except for extreme liberals. While some significant effects are found at lower levels of polarization, the pattern of effects present a more coherent picture at higher levels. With evidence that pork is related to general spending attitudes and that this link appears to strengthen with polarization, the discussion now continues to the effects of pork on voting behavior.

The Pork Barrel and Voting Behavior

A survey of the literature on distributive benefits yields few empirical analyses that focus on individual constituents. The overwhelming majority of the empirical work on distributive benefits is conducted at the district level. Even the theoretical work has only addressed the preferences of individuals to justify predictions of universalism in the distribution of benefits (Niou and Ordeshook 1985; Shepsle and Weingast 1981; Weingast, Shepsle, and Johnsen 1981). Given the prediction that representatives want as large a share of the pork barrel as they can secure, it must be that the representative derives an electoral benefit from this spending. Distributive projects are representative of district service that can be credited to the incumbent when she seeks reelection (Cain, Ferejohn, and Fiorina 1987; Grimmer, Messing, and Westwood 2012; Mayhew 1974). If it is assumed that representatives seek benefits for their electoral effects, it must also be assumed that voters generally prefer more spending in their districts.

These assumptions about the individual are built into the empirical models of those who have looked at voters as opposed to district-level outcomes. Few works have directly estimated the effect of distributive benefits or related variables on individual attitudes and behavior. Several early works consider the impact of pork as casework. Johannes and McAdams (1981) report null effects of casework on voting for the incumbent, with Johannes (1980, 1983a) finding that the distribution of casework is largely idiosyncratic or more a function of constituent expectations (1983b), but Fiorina (1981) concludes that correcting the methodological flaws in their work reveals a positive relationship between casework and incumbent support. Cain, Ferejohn, and Fiorina (1987) reach similar conclusions regarding the relationship between casework and voting. Grimmer, Messing, and Westwood (2012) provide another direct test of credit claiming, finding that constituents are responsive to credit-claiming messages. Different from the direct influence of casework, they argue that legislators use credit-claiming messages to shape constituent views of what the legislator has done and how closely the legislator is tied to spending. Further, they report that constituents respond to the number of credit-claiming messages and not the amount of spending for which legislators claim credit.

Beyond the research on casework, a number of works have directly estimated the effects of spending on the likelihood of voting for the incumbent. Stein and Bickers (1994a), arguably the best known of these works, found that pork has strong effects on voter awareness of incumbent activities and weak direct effects on incumbent favorability and voting. Stronger indirect effects of pork on voting exist through awareness and favorability. Sellers (1997) also reports a positive relationship between pork and voting for Senate incumbents, but the relationship is conditioned by the perceived fiscal ideology of the incumbent, with only those who are fiscally liberal or moderate benefiting electorally from the pork barrel. There are also significant relationships beyond voting for congressional incumbents. Chen (2013), for example, observes a relationship between disaster aid in Florida and turnout in the 2004 elections (favoring Republicans).

Missing from all of these works is a test of the assumption that voters reward distributive activities equally. One such test can be found in a study by Kriner and Reeves (2012), who found that an increase in pork in a voter's congressional district increased the likelihood of voting for John McCain in 2008 for all but the most conservative voters. While several works analyzing the district or state level suggest an ideological difference in voter reactions to the pork barrel (Alvarez and Saving 1997b; Bickers and Stein 2000; Crespin and Finocchiaro 2013; Lazarus and Reilly 2010), Kriner and Reeves (2012) is the only published work I could find offering a quantitative model that conditions the effects of pork on the ideological identification of the voter. Two other works, both conference papers, also find that conservative voters may punish representatives for pork barreling. Bickers et al. (2007), examining the 2006 elections, report a decreasing likelihood of voting for Republican incumbents among conservative voters as credit claiming for pork increases. Sidman and Mak (2006) reach a similar conclusion looking at the 2004 elections, finding that politically sophisticated conservatives are the least likely to vote for pork barreling Republicans.

The foregoing discussion of ideology, the findings with respect to attitudes, and the results of the few works that condition the effects of pork on voter ideology suggest several hypotheses relevant to this examination. First, liberal voters should generally reward incumbents for securing distributive spending and penalize incumbents who secure contingent liabilities. Second, we should observe the opposite for conservative voters. Moderate voters have largely been ignored in this discussion of ideology. Ellis and Stimson (2012) report that a large majority of respondents over time hold preferences for increasing spending on several items that would be considered distributive. From this I assume that moderates will generally reward all types of pork barreling, lacking an ideological reflex in opposition to certain types of programs. Given that increasing polarization was found to accentuate the effects of the pork barrel, both in terms of aggregate electoral effects and preferences for less government spending, these relationships are expected to be statistically significant only at higher levels of polarization.

Data and Methods

Voting behavior is examined using the same ANES data as were used for the analyses of spending attitudes. The analysis includes all of the years in the cumulative data file for which data on the pork barrel are available: 1986 through 2012, excluding 2006 and 2010. The dependent variable is dichotomous, coded 1 if the respondent voted for the incumbent and 0 if the respondent voted for the challenger. Nonvoters are excluded from the analysis. The likelihood of voting for the incumbent is estimated using probit, adjusting standard errors for clustering by election year and including the appropriate survey weights. Distributive spending and contingent liability awards are measured as before, as is polarization. To examine the interplay between these two variables and voter ideology, ideology is interacted with both measures of the pork barrel and with polarization. The three-way ideology-pork-polarization interactions are included as well. Ideology is measured as it was in the spending-preferences analysis, using a five-point scale with dummy variables for liberal, moderate, conservative, and extremely conservative (extremely liberal is the excluded category).

The model controls for several variables that appeared in the most-important-problem and spending-preferences analyses. The likelihood of voting for the incumbent is modeled as a function of gender (female), race (black), income percentile, education level, party identification, and economic retrospections. There are, however, some differences from the previous models. Given the propensity of women, blacks, those in lower income categories, and those of lower educational attainment to vote Democratic, each of those variables is interacted with a dummy variable coded 1 for Democratic incumbents. Income percentile and education level are also included here as continuous variables, not categorical as in the previous models. Party identification, measured using dummy variables for Democratic and Republican identifiers, is also interacted with incumbent party. Expecting that members of the president's party will be rewarded for economic improvement, economic retrospections are interacted with a dummy variable coded 1 for members of the president's party.

Additionally, the four district-level variables from the most-important-problem analysis are included: whether the incumbent ran in a contested primary, whether the general-election challenger has held an elected office, the natural log of challenger spending, and the natural log of incumbent spending. All four are expected to have negative relationships with voting for the incumbent. The final control variable included is the ideological difference between the incumbent and the district and the interactions of this variable with polarization and the ideological identification of the voter. Ideological difference, measured as the residuals of an OLS regression of incumbent DW-NOMINATE scores on the district-level vote share of the Republican presidential candidate in the most recent election (Brady, Han, and Pope 2007), is discussed in greater detail in the next chapter. It is included as a measure of how conservative the incumbent is relative to the district. It is expected that liberals will penalize increasing conservatism, conservatives will reward it, and both sets of effects will increase in magnitude and statistical strength with polarization. As polarization increases, ideological differences are expected to become more relevant to voters.

Vote Choice Results

Model estimates are presented in table 4.3. As with the previous analyses in this chapter, the results are best discussed in terms of predicted probabilities and, for the pork barrel, marginal effects. The control variables affect the likelihood of voting for the incumbent largely as expected. Looking first at demographic characteristics, the likelihood of voting for Democratic incumbents and against Republican incumbents tends to increase for women, blacks, and voters in lower income percentiles. With respect to education, moving from the lowest category to the highest produces a decrease in the predicted probability of voting for Republican

Table 4.3
Vote Choice Results

Variable	Coefficient	Std. Err.
Ideology (Extremely liberal excluded)		
Liberal	−0.095	0.528
x Polarization	0.817	0.864
x Distributive spending	−1.825*	0.629
x Polarization x DS	1.937†	0.997
x Contingent liabilities	0.076	0.765
x Polarization x CL	−0.599	1.523
x Ideological difference	3.017†	1.546
x Polarization x ID	−4.036†	2.359
Moderate	0.338	0.488
x Polarization	−0.453	0.813
x Distributive spending	−1.973*	0.706
x Polarization x DS	2.498*	1.088
x Contingent liabilities	0.158	0.589
x Polarization x CL	−0.591	1.149
x Ideological difference	5.025*	1.723
x Polarization x ID	−6.136*	2.619
Conservative	0.490	0.478
x Polarization	−1.156	0.836
x Distributive spending	−1.767*	0.779
x Polarization x DS	1.974†	1.170
x Contingent liabilities	−0.007	0.665
x Polarization x CL	−0.240	1.358
x Ideological difference	5.345*	1.993
x Polarization x ID	−4.176	2.980
Extreme Conservative	0.498	0.495
x Polarization	−1.294	0.860
x Distributive spending	−2.163*	0.779
x Polarization x DS	2.171†	1.127
x Contingent liabilities	0.162	0.835
x Polarization x CL	−0.336	1.627
x Ideological difference	4.771*	2.151
x Polarization x ID	−4.267	3.385
Polarization	0.011	0.869
Distributive spending	1.972*	0.625
x Polarization	−2.396*	0.944

Table 4.3 *(Continued)*

Variable	Coefficient	Std. Err.
Contingent liabilities	0.056	0.651
x Polarization	0.112	1.310
Ideological difference	−5.074*	1.838
x Polarization	5.783*	2.725
Contested primary	−0.113†	0.067
Experienced challenger	−0.055	0.060
ln(Challenger spending)	−0.018†	0.010
ln(Incumbent spending)	−0.176*	0.038
Democratic incumbent	−0.254	0.178
President's party	−0.031	0.094
Female	−0.062†	0.037
x Democratic incumbent	0.151†	0.082
Black	−0.663*	0.207
x Democratic incumbent	1.268*	0.211
Income percentile	0.103*	0.040
x Democratic incumbent	−0.124*	0.048
Education level	−0.071*	0.034
x Democratic incumbent	0.068	0.052
Democrat	−0.937*	0.074
x Democratic incumbent	1.803*	0.091
Republican	1.015*	0.109
x Democratic incumbent	−1.792	0.140
Economic retrospections	−0.256	0.101
x President's party	0.611	0.226
Intercept	3.160	0.558
Model statistics		
Observations	6,957	
Log Pseudolikelihood	−2,851.915	
LR χ^2 (9)	3,073.735*	
% Correctly predicted	81.4%	

Source: Author's analysis of data from American National Election Studies (2015), Bonica (2013), U.S. Bureau of the Census (n.d.), and U.S. Bureau of Fiscal Service (2019).

* p < 0.05 (two-tailed)

† p < 0.05 (one-tailed, directional hypothesis expected)

Note: The model is estimated via probit. The dependent variable is coded 1 if the respondent voted for the incumbent, 0 if the respondent voted for the major-party challenger. Standard errors are adjusted for clustering by election year.

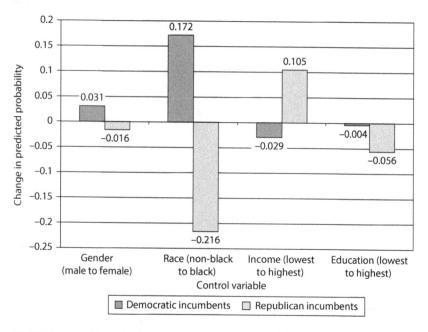

FIGURE 4.3 **Effects of control variables on the probability of voting for the incumbent** The change in predicted probability of voting for the incumbent is the difference moving from the first value in the parenthetical (e.g., the lowest income percentile) to the second value (e.g., the highest income percentile). Predicted probabilities are calculated holding polarization, both pork barrel measures, incumbent-district ideological difference, and candidate spending at their means. Other variables are set to the following values: uncontested primary, amateur challenger, moderate identifier, male, nonblack, Independent, income in the 34th through 67th percentile, high school graduate, belief that the national economy has gotten worse, Democratic incumbent, and Republican president. *Source*: Author's analysis of data from American National Election Studies (2015), Bonica (2013a), U.S. Bureau of the Census (n.d.), and U.S. Bureau of Fiscal Service (2019).

incumbents, but the effect on voting for Democratic incumbents is negligible. These effects are depicted in figure 4.3. Economic evaluations have a substantial impact on voting in House elections. When voters evaluate the economy as worse than one year ago, there is a decrease of 0.208 in the predicted probability of voting for incumbents from the president's party. This probability increases by 0.176 when voters believe the economy has improved.

Turning to aggregate phenomena, three of the four campaign-related variables significantly decrease the likelihood of voting for the incumbent. This chapter has not presented much information regarding the costs of running in a contested primary, which is partly the focus of the next chapter. Goodliffe and Magleby (2001) found that incumbents running in competitive primaries tend to suffer in the general election. That conclusion is supported here. The presence of a contested primary decreases the predicted probability of voting for the incumbent in the general election by 0.04. Increases in challenger spending and incumbent spending, consistent with Jacobson (1990), also decrease the likelihood of voting for the incumbent. An increase of one standard deviation in each decreases the probability of voting for the incumbent by 0.028 and 0.052, respectively. Finally, the effects of ideological difference between the incumbent and the district show that liberal, extremely liberal, and moderate voters tend to punish increasing conservatism relative to the district while conservatives and extreme conservatives reward these shifts.

The Pork Barrel and Voting Behavior

Figure 4.4 presents the marginal effects of distributive spending on the voting behavior of extreme liberals, conservatives, and extreme conservatives. These are the only categories of ideology for which significant effects were found. Put another way, the empirical links between distributive spending and voting behavior are far weaker for liberal and moderate voters. Considering the three types of voters for whom distributive spending is significant, the effects are largely as expected: extreme liberals are more likely to vote for pork barreling incumbents, and conservatives of both categories are less likely to vote for such incumbents. The results for conservatives and extreme conservatives are the most supportive of the argument that the pork barrel becomes more relevant as polarization increases. As figure 4.4 demonstrates, the marginal effect of distributive spending is only significant at higher levels of polarization for conservatives and extreme conservatives. When polarization is very high—a value of 0.8, for example—an increase of one standard deviation in distributive spending decreases the probability of

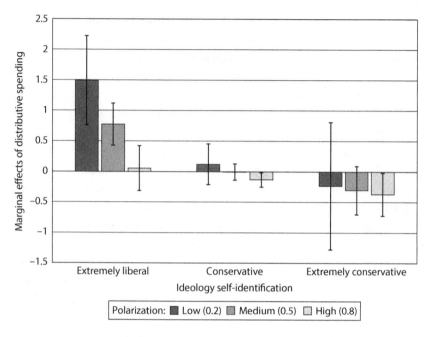

FIGURE 4.4 **Marginal effects of distributive spending on vote choice**
Ideology is measured using five categories, but only the three for which significant effects are observed are presented here. Error bars represent 90 percent confidence intervals. *Source*: Author's analysis of data from American National Election Studies (2015), Bonica (2013a), U.S. Bureau of the Census (n.d.), and U.S. Bureau of Fiscal Service (2019).

voting for the incumbent by 0.028 and 0.08 for conservatives and extreme conservatives, respectively. The effects are larger for extreme liberals, but decrease in magnitude as polarization increases. Even so, increases in distributive spending significantly increase the likelihood of extreme liberals' voting for the incumbent across the range of polarization, except when polarization is at its highest levels. While the marginal effect is not significant when polarization is close to its maximum, as depicted in figure 4.4, it is significant at a still high value of 0.7. At this level, an increase of one standard deviation in distributive spending increases the probability of voting for the incumbent by 0.055. To complete the discussion of extremely liberal voters, when polarization is low—a value of 0.2, for example—increasing distributive spending by one standard deviation increases the probability of voting for the incumbent by 0.23. The increase in probability is a still substantial 0.135 when polarization is at a middling level of 0.5.

Contingent liabilities generally do not have a direct influence on voting behavior in these results. The one exception is for self-identified liberals (not extreme liberals). Here, as was seen for conservatives and overall distributive spending, the effects are consistent with expectations. Specifically, an increase in contingent liability awards decreases the likelihood of voting for the incumbent. The negative effect of contingent liability awards also grows in magnitude as polarization increases and is significant at higher, but not lower, levels of polarization. When polarization is equal to 0.44, the lowest value for which contingent liabilities are significant, an increase of one standard deviation in contingent liability awards decreases the probability of voting for the incumbent by 0.027. When polarization increases to 0.8, the decrease in probability almost triples (to 0.074).

Neither distributive spending nor contingent liability awards significantly affect the behavior of moderate voters. In arguing that reactions to the pork barrel are grounded in ideology, I expect that the strongest reactions to the pork barrel will be among those voters who identify as either liberal or conservative. If the pork barrel is an ideological issue, and if its effects become less idiosyncratic, more tied to ideology and party, and stronger in magnitude as political polarization increases, then it is unsurprising that the effects are largely null for those who are truly moderate or unwilling to place themselves on either the left or the right ideologically.

Conclusion

The previous chapter established a link between the pork barrel and election outcomes that stretches back at least to the period immediately after the end of Reconstruction. Consistent with expectations that can be derived from recent work on the pork barrel, there are different and predictable partisan effects of the pork barrel. Democratic incumbents benefit from public-works spending, and the electoral fortunes of Republican incumbents are harmed by this spending. Most importantly for my theory, the magnitude of these effects varies with political polarization, strengthening when polarization is high and attenuating when polarization is low. Throughout this work so far, I have argued that reactions to the pork barrel are grounded in ideology. The pork barrel, in its classical, project-based spending incarnation, is a central aspect of New Deal liberalism and anathema to modern conservatism. Conservatives, on the other hand, favor government actions and spending that promote private behavior. The previous chapter discussed the historical development of the pork barrel in an ideological context, and this chapter presents the empirical evidence for links between the pork barrel, attitudes, and behavior.

The products of distributive spending are visible, publicized in the media and by interest groups and local opinion leaders, and touted by credit-claiming members of Congress. While it is doubtful that average people know exactly how much federal money is spent in their communities, the conditions exist for them to have a sense of whether their districts are receiving more or less funding, relatively speaking. Here, then, is the first empirical link between pork and attitudes presented in this chapter. Increases in in-district distributive spending lead to an increase in the probability that individuals will cite government spending as the most important problem facing the country. Government spending is rarely offered as the most important problem, but the likelihood of its mention increases when more distributive spending happens in respondents' communities. There is, therefore, a systematic relationship between the pork barrel and general spending attitudes. Ideology and polarization were not included in that analysis, but these factors condition the relationship between pork and preferences for government spending. Particularly in high-polarization environments, increases in distributive spending lead conservatives and extreme conservatives to favor less government spending. Liberals, on the other hand, become far more likely to prefer spending at current or higher levels. Finally, the expected links between pork, polarization, and behavior are observed in the context of House elections. When polarization is elevated and distributive spending increases, conservatives and extreme conservatives are less likely to vote for their

House incumbents. Extreme liberals are more likely to do so. Those identifying simply as liberal are more responsive to contingent liability awards, becoming less likely to vote for incumbents as awards increase, starting from moderate levels of polarization.

Partisan effects for different types of pork barrel spending are not new to the literature. This chapter, however, accomplishes two things relatively absent from the literature that inform the subsequent analyses and discussions in this book. First, the chapter presents empirical support for an ideology-based theory of the electoral effects of the pork barrel. Individuals react differently to the pork barrel depending on the type of spending, the level of polarization in the partisan public, and their own ideological identification. These factors influence attitudes about government spending generally and the voting behavior of individuals. Knowing, for example, that when polarization is high, conservatives will develop stronger preferences for reducing government spending and penalize representatives securing "too much" distributive spending might lead strategic actors, such as potential challengers and campaign donors, to behave differently. The behavior of these actors has, as the next few chapters demonstrate, serious implications for the outcomes of House elections. Second, the analysis of voting behavior provides empirical support for an ideological basis for the differential partisan effects observed in other studies. Democrats tend to benefit electorally from distributive spending, and Republicans do not. While previous work has speculated that an ideological reaction among voters exists, there is scant evidence of this phenomenon. Moving forward, we can explain the direct electoral costs and benefits of pork barreling at least partially in terms of how the preferences of core constituencies (conservatives for Republicans and liberals for Democrats) translate into vote shares at the district level.

5

Challenges from Within the Party

ON JUNE 10, 2014, House Majority Leader Eric Cantor lost his primary election to David Brat, an economics professor at Randolph-Macon College. Brat's win sent shock waves through American politics. Cantor was the first sitting House majority leader to lose a primary since creation of the position in 1899 (Lipman 2014). Cantor's loss was unusual not only because he was the House majority leader. The simple fact is that House incumbents almost *never* lose primary elections. Cantor's loss was likely the result of a confluence of extraordinary factors: his stance on the very salient issue of immigration; his status as majority leader, making him emblematic of Washington insiders; and the substantial support given to his challenger by conservative media personalities. Cantor's 2014 primary is a prominent example of why this chapter focuses on primary competition rather than defeat. Defeat is very rare and tends to be idiosyncratic to the dynamics of particular races. Few factors, like scandal or severe ideologically inconsistency between the member and primary voters, offer general explanations for the loss of incumbents in primary elections. Primary competition, on the other hand, is not an infrequent occurrence, it is systematically related to several variables generally important to understanding congressional elections, and it has serious consequences for general election outcomes.

Despite the success rate of incumbents in primaries, given the potential costs of running in a competitive primary, any rational incumbent would prefer to secure the nomination unopposed. Even when facing weak challengers, incumbents spend resources and risk the early revelation of damaging information during these contests. This chapter demonstrates the roles played by polarization and the pork barrel in primary contestation, showing that the pork barrel affects whether Republican incumbents are opposed in primary elections, particularly when polarization is elevated. Much like increasing incumbent liberalism relative to the district, securing more distributive (i.e., "liberal") spending opens Republicans up to potential challenges. The results have important implications for elections because, as will be discussed in chapter 7, incumbents running in contested primaries perform significantly worse in the general election.

Importance of Primary Elections

The obvious importance of primary elections lies in their function as candidate-selection mechanisms. Very few third-party candidates are elected to Congress, and this has been especially true over the past forty years. Winning a major-party nomination is, therefore, a necessary first step in being elected to Congress. Incumbents tend to occupy a privileged position here. As noted in the beginning of this chapter, incumbent losses in primary elections are exceptionally rare. Between 1986 and 2012, the time span analyzed in this and successive chapters, only sixty-six House incumbents have lost primaries, and 48.5 percent of those losses occurred in just two election years: 1992 (nineteen defeats) and 2012 (thirteen defeats).[1] Over that same period, there were 5,481 reelection contests, and according to data from the Federal Election Commission (Bonica 2013a), 1,512 of those featured a contested primary. Putting the numbers together, incumbents lost 4.4 percent of the time when challenged in the primary, and only 1.2 percent of the time when the denominator is all reelection contests. Another important aspect of House primary elections is that they are ubiquitous. From 1986 to 2012, only twelve

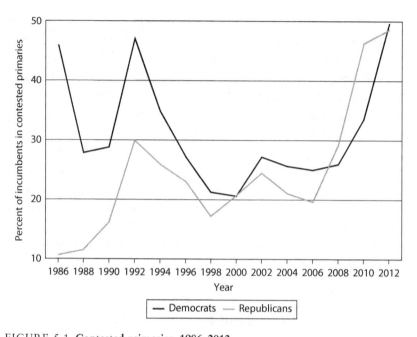

FIGURE 5.1 **Contested primaries, 1986–2012**
Curves depict the percentage of incumbents from each party facing at least one challenger in the primary election. *Source*: Bonica (2013a)

reelection contests did not feature a primary. The overwhelming majority of incumbents simply run unopposed. This can be seen in figure 5.1, which graphs the percentage of primary elections by party that were contested. From a legal perspective, running in a primary makes sense for the incumbent. Not only do state party organizations have rules governing candidate selection, but primaries are separate elections and therefore allow candidates to collect double the amount in contributions as would be permitted for the general election alone. While having primaries carries fund-raising benefits, the existence of a primary, rather than other candidate-selection mechanisms, could entice disaffected constituents or other ambitious individuals to challenge the incumbent for the party's nomination. Despite the extraordinary success rate of House incumbents in primaries, incumbents have an interest in running unopposed for their party's nomination.

A number of studies have found that the level of primary competition has implications for general-election campaigns. Goodliffe and Magleby (2001) report that the general-election vote share of incumbents who faced competitive primaries—which they define as primary elections in which the margin of victory is within twenty points—is more than ten points lower than that of incumbents running in unopposed or weakly competitive primaries. Born (1981) reaches similar conclusions in substance, if not magnitude. Lazarus (2005) reports a similar general-election cost for Democratic incumbents as their primary-election victory margin decreases and, for all incumbents, a negative relationship between the number of primary challengers and general-election vote share. Kenney (1988), however, found no relationship between primary divisiveness and general-election outcomes in 1984 House elections. The deleterious effects of contested primaries are not confined to direct effects on general-election vote share. A number of studies suggest indirect effects, with contested primaries depleting the campaign resources of incumbents. Goodliffe and Magleby (2001) found that incumbents running in competitive primaries spent almost twice as much as incumbents in weakly competitive primaries. Ezra (2001), using data from interviews, discusses the perceived benefits and drawbacks of primary campaigns. Campaigns with more political capital, such as incumbent reelection campaigns, tend to view primaries as harmful, citing the drain on campaign resources in particular. Conversely, the perceived benefits (e.g., improved organization, publicity, legitimacy) tend to accrue to candidates with less political capital. Adams and Merrill (2008) reach a similar conclusion in a formal model of two-stage elections.

Ideology and Primaries

The anecdote from the introduction to this chapter hints at a divergence between primary and general electorates. Whereas general electorates are assumed to be moderate, pushing candidates toward a centrist position (Black 1958; Downs 1957), primary electorates, especially in congressional elections, are generally assumed to be more interested in politics, more knowledgeable about the record of the incumbent, and more likely to hold positions that are more extreme (or at least more consistent with respect to ideology) than the general electorate (Burden 2001). This extreme primary electorate has been blamed, in part, for the increase in polarization in Congress (Fiorina, Abrams, and Pope 2006), although McGhee et al. (2014) suggest that polarization may result not from the electorate per se, but from the donors and activists who support candidates (see also Green 2001). Recognizing the differing preferences of these two constituencies, candidates could try appealing to an extreme electorate to win the nomination and then moderating those positions when campaigning in the general election (Turbowitz and Mellow 2005). Despite the perceived negative relationship between ideological extremity and general-election outcomes (Canes-Wrone, Brady, and Cogan 2002), Burden (2001, 2004) argues that the shift from extreme to moderate is not costless. Fiorina, Abrams, and Pope (2006) also suggest redistricting reform as a means of reducing elite polarization. The logic here is that gerrymandered districts heavily favor one party, making the primary election, with its extreme constituency, more important for winning election to Congress than the moderate general-election constituency. This logic can be extended to legislators' targeting distributive benefits to these more extreme primary voters (Hirano, Snyder, and Ting 2009).

These works examine the polarizing effects of primary elections, predicated on the role that candidate ideology plays in their outcomes. That primary electorates tend toward the extremes is not enough to produce these results. It must also be that these voters prefer extremity to moderation in the positions taken by candidates vying for their party's nomination. On this point, the empirical evidence is convincing. Brady, Han, and Pope (2007) find that ideological extremity is beneficial to incumbents in primary elections similar to moderation in general elections (Canes-Wrone, Brady, and Cogan 2002). Democrats who are more liberal and Republicans who are more conservative than their districts face fewer primary challengers and win by larger margins. Related to this, Dominguez (2011) finds that endorsements from partisan groups and individuals significantly increase the likelihood of winning primaries and candidates' vote shares. Tying this to ideology, one could assume that these endorsements, especially from endorsers whose politics are easy to identify (e.g., the National Organization for Women, the Tea Party) convey information about the ideological positions of the candidate.

In order for primary elections to contribute to polarization, it has to be the case that ideological extremity is rewarded in primaries. Brady, Han, and Pope (2007) provide empirical support for this argument, showing that extremity reduces the number of primary challengers to, and increases the primary election vote share of, the incumbent. What is true of general ideological positions should also be true of the pork barrel specifically, particularly during periods of high polarization. In the previous chapter, I noted that the pork barrel becomes more relevant to one's general attitudes regarding government spending as polarization increases. We should, therefore, observe effects of the pork barrel that are more ideologically consistent and systematic when polarization is high. This should also be true of general ideological positions. Assuming that the primary electorate is indeed more interested and more informed and tends to hold opinions that are more extreme, it is expected that increases in total distributive spending will be harmful to Republican incumbents and beneficial to Democratic incumbents. Increases in contingent liability awards should have the opposite effects. Given the role that ideological differences between the incumbent and the district are expected to play in primary-election outcomes, it is important to control for these effects; the pork barrel and general ideological differences are related, but the pork barrel should have effects beyond working through evaluations of overall ideology.

Data and Methods

The dependent variable is dichotomous, coded 1 if the incumbent ran in a contested primary election, 0 if the incumbent was unopposed.[2] The likelihood of a contested primary is estimated with a probit model, adjusting standard errors for clustering by election year. Contested primaries are modeled as a function of both pork barrel measures and their interaction with the party of the incumbent and polarization. Distributive spending is expected to have ideologically consistent effects in primary elections, just as it had on aggregate election outcomes. An increase in distributive spending is expected to increase the likelihood that a Republican incumbent will face a primary challenger and decrease the likelihood for Democratic incumbents. Opposite effects are expected for contingent liability awards, with Republican incumbents less likely and Democratic incumbents more likely to face a primary challenge as awards increase. With respect to polarization, the effects of distributive spending and contingent liability awards are expected to increase in magnitude as polarization increases, with statistical significance found at higher but not lower levels of polarization.

Control Variables

The effects of ideological congruence between the legislator and constituents are not a central focus of this work, but I treat it here as more than a typical control variable. Rather than an absolute measure of positions, the analysis includes a measure of legislator positions relative to the district. Brady, Han, and Pope (2007), examining competition in primary elections, measure legislator-district congruence using the residuals of a regression of member first-dimension DW-NOMINATE scores on district preferences, measured by the proportion of the vote received by the Republican candidate in the most recent presidential election. I estimate that model using data from 1980 through 2012 via ordinary least squares, producing the following results:

$$DW\text{-}NOMINATE_{it} = -0.929 + 1.913 \times Republican\ Pres.Vote\ Share_{it}$$

$$\left(N = 7,385; \bar{R} = 0.365\right)$$

The standard errors of the intercept and the coefficient on Republican presidential candidate vote share are 0.015 and 0.029, respectively. The measurement strategy has several benefits. First, it does not require that both measures of preferences be on the same scale. Second, it employs a measure of district preferences, presidential vote share (Erikson and Wright 1980), that has been widely accepted by scholars of Congress for decades. Third, as opposed to using only a measure of absolute ideological position for the member, the residual measures the ideological position of the member relative to the district. Fourth, the residuals have a meaning substantively important to the study of congressional elections. Positive residuals imply that the member is more conservative than the district; negative residuals imply the member is more liberal.

The measure is thus referred to here as one of ideological difference between the legislator and constituents. Directionality was important in the Brady, Han, and Pope (2007) investigation, and it is important here. Like the pork barrel measures, ideological difference is interacted with incumbent party and polarization. The variable is a measure of incumbent conservatism relative to the district. This will naturally have different implications for Democrats and Republicans. Just as I have argued with respect to the pork barrel, ideological difference should also matter more as polarization increases. Ideological difference is expected to increase the likelihood of a primary challenge for Democratic incumbents and decrease this likelihood for Republican incumbents, consistent with the findings of Brady, Han, and Pope (2007).

The model includes additional control variables, drawn from previous studies of congressional primary elections (e.g., Brady, Han, and Pope 2007; Carson et al. 2012; Lazarus 2005), accounting for political conditions and characteristics of the states. Political conditions are measured using five variables and one interaction. First, I include the partisan normal vote, measured as the mean district vote share for the incumbent's party in the past three presidential elections. Increases in the normal vote, signifying partisan conditions more favorable to the incumbent party, are expected to increase the likelihood of a contested primary, given that the incumbent party will be more favored in the general election, making that party's nomination a more attractive prize to potential candidates (Stone, Maisel, and Maestas 2004). Second, I include the incumbent's general-election vote share in the previous election. Lagged incumbent general-election vote share should have effects opposite to those of the normal vote. Increases here imply that the incumbent occupies a safe position and is likely of higher quality (Herrnson and Gimpel 1995; Stone, Maisel, and Maestas 2004).[3] The third variable is seniority, measured as the number of terms, including the current term, that the incumbent has served in the House. Seniority is expected to decrease the likelihood of a contested primary because senior members have had more time with their primary constituencies (Brady, Han, and Pope 2007; Fenno 1978). The fourth variable is a dummy variable indicating membership in the president's party. Fifth is the annualized percent change in real gross domestic product (RGDP) for the second quarter., Finally,

I include the interaction between the previous two variables. The interaction of RGDP change and presidential partisanship is expected to behave like lagged general-election vote share, with economic improvement benefiting incumbents from the party of the president and decreasing the likelihood of a contested primary.

I use four dummy variables to measure state-based factors expected to affect primary-election competition. First, a dummy variable is included for southern states, as defined by the U.S. Census Bureau; this variable is interacted with a dummy variable indicating whether the incumbent is a Democrat, expecting that Democrats in general, and southern Democrats in particular, are more likely to face primary opposition (Jewell and Breaux 1991; Schantz 1980). Second, I include a dummy variable for closed-primary states, which are expected to decrease the likelihood of contested primaries (Herrnson and Gimpel 1995).[4] Third is a dummy variable indicating that a state has term limits for state legislators (who thus become ineligible to seek reelection), which is expected to increase the likelihood of a contested primary.[5] Powell (2000) and Steen (2006) find a positive correlation between term limits and state legislators' running for the House, with Steen (2006) adding that significant effects are specific to state legislators who have exhausted their terms of service, not those for whom term limits loom on the horizon. The final variable included is an indicator for the redistricting years of 1992, 2002, and 2012. I expect there to be a greater proportion of contested primaries as states redraw boundary lines, potentially changing constituencies familiar to the incumbent (Brady, Han, and Pope 2007; Schantz 1980).

Results

Figure 5.1, earlier in this chapter, shows that Democratic incumbents are more likely overall to run in contested primaries. This was particularly true throughout the 1980s and is at least partially explained by the results presented in table 5.1. Specifically, southern Republicans are less likely and southern Democrats are slightly more likely to run in contested primaries. Throughout the 1980s, House delegations in southern states had not yet fully transitioned from solid Democrat to solid Republican.

Table 5.1

Probit Estimates for the Likelihood of a Contested Primary

Variable	Coefficient	Std. Err.
Democrat	1.322*	0.409
Polarization	2.408*	0.377
x Democrat	−2.636*	0.813
Distributive spending	−0.109	0.083
x Democrat	−0.021	0.177
x Polarization	0.270*	0.106
x Polarization x Democrat	−0.088	0.217
Contingent liability awards	0.202	0.161
x Democrat	−0.228	0.227
x Polarization	−0.212	0.243
x Polarization x Democrat	0.284	0.345
Ideological difference	0.483	0.442
x Democrat	−0.509	0.538
x Polarization	−1.358	0.833
x Polarization x Democrat	2.223*	1.113
Normal vote	1.494*	0.204
Lagged incumbent vote share	−0.446*	0.213
President's party	0.667*	0.334
RGDP Q2	0.076	0.049
x President's party	−0.218*	0.085
Seniority	0.013*	0.006
Southern state	−0.333*	0.080
x Democrat	0.382*	0.123
Closed primary	−0.281*	0.063
Term limits	−0.115	0.066
Redistricting year	0.263*	0.060
Intercept	−2.463*	0.359
Model statistics		
Observations	5,312	
Log Pseudolikelihood	−2,949.999	
LR $\chi^2_{(12)}$	364.542*	
Percent correctly predicted	73.1%	

Source: Author's analysis of data from American National Election Studies (2007, 2011, 2015), Bonica (2013), Lewis et al. (2019), National Conference of State Legislatures (2015, 2018), U.S. Bureau of the Census (n.d.), U.S. Bureau of Economic Analysis (2018), and U.S. Bureau of Fiscal Service (2019).

* $p < 0.05$ (two-tailed)

Note: Standard errors are adjusted for clustering by election year.

By the end of the decade, nearly every southern state still had Democrats constituting more than 50 percent of its House delegation. Seniority may also be a culprit here, as it is positively correlated to primary contestation. In the time period examined here, mean seniority is always greater for Democrats than for Republicans, but in the decade of the 1980s, Democrats had their largest share of House seats (60.5 percent), as compared to their share in 1990s (54.5 percent) or the twenty-first century (50.8 percent), exacerbating the gap between Democrats and Republicans during that decade. Additionally, members of the president's party are less likely to face primary opposition as the economy grows. The boom times of the 1980s also played a role in the size of the gap, which would largely close during the boom times of the Clinton era. Figure 5.2 graphically presents the effects of statistically significant control variables, discussed in the next paragraph, on the predicted probability of a contested primary.

The effects of political conditions are calculated, holding all other variables constant,[6] for increases of one standard deviation in the relevant variables. The effects of state characteristics, which are all dichotomous, are presented as the change in predicted probability of a contested primary resulting from the presence, relative to the absence, of each characteristic. Starting from the left end of figure 5.2, an 11.3-point increase in the partisan normal vote causes a 0.06 increase in the predicted probability of a contested primary. Conversely, a 15.4-point increase in the lagged general-election vote share of the incumbent decreases the probability of a contested primary by 0.023. Incumbents are, therefore, more likely to be challenged in the primary when political conditions in the district are more favorable to their party, but less likely to be challenged if their position is relatively safe. Related effects are observed for increases in real gross domestic product. The probability that members of the president's party, who would presumably benefit from economic improvement when their party occupies the White House, face a contested primary decreases 0.092 for a 2.127 percent increase in second quarter RGDP. For members of the opposition party, the same increase in RGDP, potentially weakening the incumbent, increases the predicted probability of a primary challenge 0.055. Interestingly, more senior members of the House are more likely to face a primary challenge. A four-term increase in seniority causes a small, but significant, 0.018 increase in the predicted probability

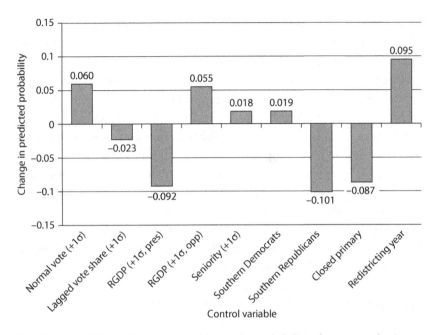

FIGURE 5.2 **Effects of control variables on the probability of a contested primary**
Bars represent the change in the predicted probability of a contested primary caused
by an increase in each of the independent variables specified on the horizontal axis.
An increase of one standard deviation from the mean is denoted (+1σ). For the annualized change in Q2 real gross domestic product, effects are presented separately for
incumbents in the president's party (Pres) and incumbents in the opposition party
(Opp). Effects for the final four variables, which are dichotomous, represent a change
from the absence of the variable to its presence. For southern Democrats, the change
is in comparison to Democrats from other regions. The same is true of southern
Republicans. The effect of closed primary rules is in comparison to states with other
rules governing voting in primary elections. Lastly, the effect of redistricting years
is in comparison to other election years. *Source*: Author's analysis of data from
American National Election Studies (2007, 2011, 2015), Bonica (2013a), Lewis et al.
(2019), National Conference of State Legislatures (2015, 2018), U.S. Bureau of the
Census (n.d.), U.S. Bureau of Economic Analysis (2018), and U.S. Bureau of Fiscal
Service (2019).

of a primary challenge. Brady, Han, and Pope (2007) find the opposite, although Lazarus (2005) reports null effects for seniority and a positive relationship between primary competition and age. The results here are a closer match to those of Lazarus, assuming that seniority is serving as a proxy for the age of the incumbent. Turning to state characteristics, the previous paragraph described the relationship between region and party. To be more specific, the predicted probability that a southern Democrat will be challenged in the primary is 0.018 greater than the probability for Democratic incumbents in other regions. The predicted probabilities for all Democrats are significantly greater than for Republicans. In rank order, southern Democrats are most likely to face a primary challenge, followed by non-southern Democrats, followed by non-southern Republicans, with southern Republicans least likely to be challenged, all else being equal. Closed primaries and redistricting years also have the expected effects on primary contestation. The probability of a contested primary in closed-primary states is 0.087 lower than in states using other rules regarding voter participation. In redistricting years, incumbents generally have a 0.095 greater probability of being challenged in the primary.

To conclude the discussion of control variables, figure 5.3 presents the effects of legislator-constituency ideological difference on primary challenges. Ideological difference behaves as expected, with increasing conservatism benefiting Republican incumbents through a reduced likelihood of primary contestation and harming Democratic incumbents. Importantly, as a test of the theory, the magnitude of the effect increases with polarization, and the effect is significant only at higher levels of polarization. Figure 5.3a presents the marginal effect (i.e., the effect of a one-unit increase) of ideological difference at three levels of polarization: low (a value of 0.2), medium (a value of 0.5), and high (a value of 0.8). Given that the hypotheses are directional, 90 percent confidence intervals accompany each marginal effect presented. The conclusions to be drawn from figure 5.3 are simple. At low levels of polarization, ideological positioning does not matter. Starting at middle levels of polarization, Democratic incumbents are more likely to be challenged in the primary when they are more conservative than are their constituents. The opposite dynamic emerges for Republican incumbents,

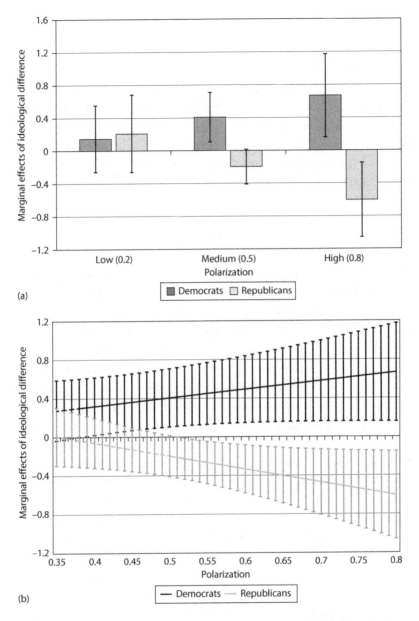

FIGURE 5.3 **Marginal effects of ideological difference on the likelihood of contested primaries**

Bars in panel (a) and lines in panel (b) represent the effect of a one-unit conservative increase in the ideological difference between legislators and their districts. Error bars are 90 percent confidence intervals. The dashed portions of curves in panel (b) depict where effects fail to reach statistical significance. *Source*: Author's analysis of data from American National Election Studies (2007, 2011, 2015), Bonica (2013a), Lewis et al. (2019), National Conference of State Legislatures (2015, 2018), U.S. Bureau of the Census (n.d.), U.S. Bureau of Economic Analysis (2018), and U.S. Bureau of Fiscal Service (2019).

but polarization needs to be a little higher before the effects are significant. Figure 5.3b shows the change in the marginal effect of ideological difference across polarization with a greater level of detail. The dashed portion of each line indicates effects that are not statistically significant. For Democrats, ideological difference is significant when polarization is greater than or equal to 0.39. For Republicans, the critical value of polarization is 0.51.

Pork and Polarization

Figure 5.4 presents the marginal effects of distributive spending on the likelihood of a contested primary. This figure is comparable in design to figure 5.3a. The marginal effects are again presented for three values of polarization (low, medium, and high) with 90 percent confidence intervals. The first observation to note, one that will be common to several of the analyses, is that the pork barrel does not significantly affect the fortunes of Democratic incumbents. I did not include a figure depicting the effects of contingent liability awards because contingent liabilities do not significantly affect primary contestation for Democrats or Republicans at any level of polarization. The same is not true of distributive spending. For Republican incumbents, the effects of distributive spending follow the pattern expected by the theory of pork as an ideological issue. The effect becomes increasingly positive as polarization rises, and the effects only become statistically significant at higher levels of polarization—specifically, 0.6. While potential Democratic primary challengers appear not to factor pork barreling into their decisions to run, Republican challengers do so when polarization is high. In the next chapter, the effects of pork on experienced general-election challengers will be described as deterrent effects. Pork barreling is an activity of the incumbent and is, therefore, something the incumbent can do to actively deter potential experienced challengers from running. The effect observed here, however, is an antideterrent, or encouragement effect. Though I am sure incumbents are not trying to encourage challengers to run in the primary, this is the effect of increasing distributive spending. For high polarization, as depicted in figure 5.4, an increase of one

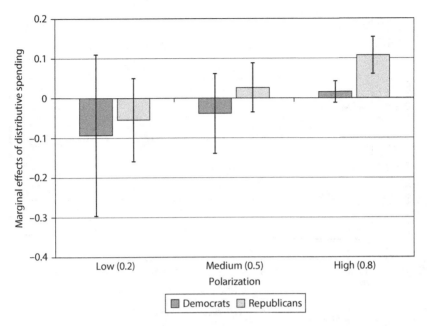

FIGURE 5.4 **Marginal effects of distributive spending on the likelihood of contested primaries**
The bars present the effect (β) of a one-unit increase in the congress-difference of real, logged distributive spending at three levels of polarization. Error bars represent 90 percent confidence intervals. *Source*: Author's analysis of data from American National Election Studies (2007, 2011, 2015), Bonica (2013a), Lewis et al. (2019), National Conference of State Legislatures (2015, 2018), U.S. Bureau of the Census (n.d.), U.S. Bureau of Economic Analysis (2018), and U.S. Bureau of Fiscal Service (2019).

standard deviation from the mean of the congress-difference in logged, real distributive spending—an increase from 0.136 to 0.546—increases the predicted probability of running in a contested primary by roughly 0.022, all else being equal. The effect is small in magnitude, but significant nonetheless.

Figure 5.5 presents the change in the predicted probability of a contested primary for both Republicans and Democrats across the effective range of distributive spending when polarization is high.[7] For Democratic incumbents, the line is essentially flat. There is a slight positive slope, but the effect is not statistically significant. For Republicans, there

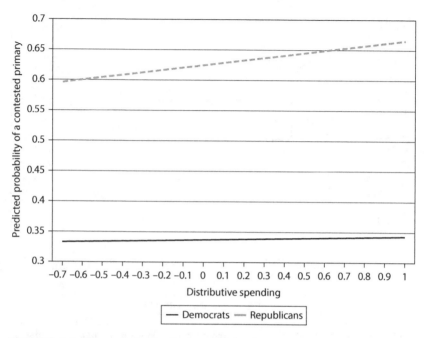

FIGURE 5.5 **Effects of distributive spending on the predicted probability of a contested primary**
Predicted probabilities are calculated holding all other variables at their mean or median values for continuous and categorical variables, respectively, except for polarization, which is held at 0.8 (high polarization). The curve for Democrats is presented for comparison purposes, but distributive spending does not significantly affect the likelihood of a contested primary for Democratic incumbents. *Source*: Author's analysis of data from American National Election Studies (2007, 2011, 2015), Bonica (2013a), Lewis et al. (2019), National Conference of State Legislatures (2015, 2018), U.S. Bureau of the Census (n.d.), U.S. Bureau of Economic Analysis (2018), and U.S. Bureau of Fiscal Service (2019).

is an increase of roughly 0.069 in the probability of a primary challenge across the effective range of distributive spending, from 0.596 to 0.665. Arguably, the most striking feature of figure 5.5 is the gap between Democrats and Republicans, a gap that is driven by heightened polarization. This can be seen in the coefficients on polarization and the polarization-incumbent party interaction in table 5.1. The effect of polarization is estimated to be 2.408; this is the effect for Republicans, all else constant.

The interactive effect subtracts 2.636 for Democrats, for a total effect of −0.228. The introduction to this chapter noted that many in the media and politics claim that Republicans seem particularly vulnerable to primary challenges. This observation is not without merit. Interestingly, the polarization effect remains even when controlling for the ideological difference between the incumbent and the district. Thus, the popular explanation of moderate incumbents' being challenged from the right may not tell the entire story. This may be a case in which the perception becomes reality.

In this era of high polarization, and especially with the rise of the Tea Party in 2010, Republican incumbents are perceived to be more vulnerable to primary challenges, despite the fact that so few incumbents lose. Believing this, potential Republican challengers are encouraged to run—even more so when the incumbent is more moderate than the district and distributive spending has increased since the previous congress. Holding all continuous variables at their means and all categorical variables at their medians, the predicted probability of a contested primary for a Republican incumbent during high polarization is 0.63. Increasing distributive spending one standard deviation and decreasing ideological difference one standard deviation (more liberal) makes that probability jump ten-and-a-half points to 0.735.

Conclusion

One observation that went without explanation above is the failure of contingent liability awards to affect the likelihood of a contested primary. Foreshadowing the results presented in the next chapter, there are null effects in the challenger experience models as well. Potential candidates in both primary and general elections do not factor contingent liabilities into their strategic calculations. One reason for this might be that contingent liabilities are less visible than direct payment and grant spending. It could also be that the nature of these programs—securing or making loans that need to be repaid or, in the case of insurance, making payments when a loss is suffered—makes them seem, falsely, less connected to voter behavior. Contingent liabilities do affect fund-raising, which implies donors are paying attention to these programs, and they have direct effects on vote share as well, suggesting a direct link to constituents. These relationships are examined in more detail in the coming chapters. Beyond contingent liabilities, distributive spending is relevant for Republicans as expected. When polarization is high, pork barreling Republicans run the risk of being challenged for the nomination. Distributive spending does not have large effects, but the results do suggest that potential Republican challengers look at distributive spending in concert with other factors such as ideology. For Democrats, it is ideology alone, and not measures of the pork barrel, that dictates primary competition.

Both here and in the literature, moderating one's positions presumably benefits the incumbent in the general election, but at the cost of increased primary competition. Under the classical view of distributive politics, these incumbents should be able to save themselves a divisive primary by bringing benefits home to the district. This, however, is not the case. For Democrats, there is simply no systematic link between pork barreling and primary competition. For Republicans, particularly when polarization is high, moderation is bad, and pork barreling, in the form of total distributive spending, makes matters worse. The irony of these results, from an ideological perspective, is that the primary challenge coming from the party's extreme will almost never succeed and, as the literature suggests and will be seen in chapter 7, will leave the incumbent in a weakened position for the general election. This increases the risk that the general-election challenger, who in all likelihood is even further away ideologically than the "moderate" incumbent, will win the seat. These general-election challengers, as well as the campaign spending of both major-party general-election candidates, are considered in the next chapter.

6

General-Election Challengers and Campaigns

THE PREVIOUS CHAPTER presents an indirect effect of the pork barrel from the standpoint of election outcomes. Republican incumbents who secure a lot of traditionally liberal pork during periods of high polarization run a greater risk of being challenged in the primary election. Previous research suggests this is harmful to the incumbent's general-election prospects, and I find the same in the next chapter. General-election challenger quality and campaign spending, the foci of this chapter, have been the subjects of many examinations of congressional elections, including both their determinants and their effects on election outcomes. On two points, the broader literature is in agreement. Experienced politicians are strategic regarding their decisions to enter congressional races. Campaign donors, too, are rational, motivated by policy goals and preferring to spend resources on candidates with greater prospects for success. Perhaps surprisingly, the indirect electoral effects of the pork barrel in this context, meaning the role of the pork barrel in determining challenger quality and campaign spending, is nearly absent from the literature. What little work exists argues the traditional perspective, which I have tied to the low-polarization context, that more pork deters the emergence of higher-quality, well-funded candidates.

I have argued that polarization conditions the effects of the pork barrel by making its ideological connections more salient, leading to partisan effects that are more consistent, more systematic, and thus more easily observed in quantitative analyses. In essence, Republican incumbents who secure "conservative" pork are safer, all else being equal, than Republicans who secure "liberal" pork.[1] The reverse is argued for Democrats. The implications of this, which are empirically tested in this chapter, are that incumbents who secure ideologically incongruous pork when polarization is high are potentially weaker than those who secure pork that is ideologically congruent with their party label (and by extension their ideological base). These weaker incumbents should be more likely to face experienced challengers, to run against challengers who spend more on their campaigns, and to be forced to spend more on their own campaigns. The results generally support these contentions, suggesting significant indirect effects of the pork barrel on election outcomes.

How Candidates and Campaigns Matter

Jacobson (1978) presents one of the earliest quantitative links between campaign spending and election outcomes. He concludes that spending is vital for the success of House challengers but indicates weakness on the part of incumbents, finding a negative relationship between incumbent campaign spending and vote share. Jacobson's rationale, which I apply here, is that incumbents will spend large quantities of campaign money only when forced to do so by the presence of well-funded challengers. Both this reasoning and the findings themselves have not gone unchallenged, and later studies have found a positive relationship between incumbent spending and vote share. Green and Krasno (1988) present the most direct evidence in conflict with Jacobson's original conclusion.[2] Positive effects have also been observed in U.S. Senate races (Abramowitz 1988; Grier 1989). A significant number of works, however, have supported the view that large amounts of spending by incumbent campaigns are either statistically unrelated to the result on Election Day or indicative of poor electoral performance (Abramowitz 1991; Basinger and Ensley 2007; Feldman and Jondrow 1984; Jacobson 1990; Levitt 1994; Ragsdale and Cook 1987). Recounting the results from the examination of vote choice in chapter 4 and foreshadowing the analyses in the next chapter, my findings are more consistent with Jacobson (1978) than the work arguing for a positive relationship between incumbent spending and vote share. Regardless of the link between incumbent spending and vote share, scholars consistently find that challengers perform better as their spending increases and that experienced or high-quality challengers are able to far outraise and outspend their amateur counterparts.

Despite the contrary findings in Jacobson (1978) and Green and Krasno (1988), both offer insights regarding the role of "quality" with respect to campaign spending and challenger performance. These and later works argue that challenger experience is vital to explaining the relationship between campaign spending and election outcomes. Experienced challengers, typically meaning those who hold or have held elected office, are of a higher quality generally (Bond, Covington, and Fleisher 1985), are able to raise more for their campaigns (Basinger and Ensley 2007), and generally perform better in elections than amateurs (Jacobson 1989), although performance differences are surely due to the strategic nature of experienced politicians in selecting races (Jacobson 1989). The current, or even former, officeholder is reluctant to spend capital, time, and potentially reputation on challenging an incumbent absent indications of incumbent weakness. The literature on candidate emergence identifies a number of factors correlated with challenger quality, including the incumbent's performance in prior elections, levels of district partisanship, challenger quality in previous elections, and the national context (Basinger and Ensley 2007; Bond, Covington, and Fleisher 1985; Carson 2005; Jacobson 1989; Krasno and Green 1988; Stone and Maisel 2003). There has been surprisingly little attention paid, however, to the relationship between challenger emergence and the pork barrel.

Bickers and Stein (1996) examined the effects of distributive benefits on the emergence of experienced challengers in the 1990 House elections. They found that increasing awards between the 100th and 101st congresses significantly decreased the likelihood that primary challengers and general-election challengers had held an elected office. The findings are one of the few pieces of statistical evidence that exists in support of what we could call a deterrent effect of the pork barrel— the type of effect posited by Mayhew (1974) in his discussion of how credit claiming advantages incumbents. Lazarus, Glas, and Barbieri (2012) also examined challenger quality, further adding an analysis of incumbent campaign receipts. Unlike Bickers and Stein (1996), the Lazarus et al. (2012) analysis was conducted in the context of earmarks during the 2008 and 2010 election cycles. Adding a partisan dynamic, they found that Democratic incumbents were able to deter the emergence of experienced primary challengers when securing earmarks. Earmarks were also positively related to campaign receipts for Democratic incumbents in 2008. Regardless of party, earmarks had no statistical relationship with general-election challenger quality in either year. While not completely contradictory, the two studies do suggest different effects of pork barrel spending, with Bickers and Stein (1996) reporting a general deterrent effect and Lazarus et al. (2012) finding the absence of such an effect in general elections. In earlier discussions of contradictory conclusions regarding the electoral effects of the pork barrel, I have suggested that results are time dependent. I argue that time dependence exists here. In 1990, a year of relatively low polarization, pork barrel spending was viewed by experienced politicians, many of whom had likely benefited from the pork barrel as state legislators (Chen 2010), as a benefit to incumbents, with the result that experienced politicians passed on challenging incumbents whose districts had received more federal spending. The elections of 2008 and 2010 were in an era of high polarization when this deterrent effect, particularly for Republicans, disappeared (or may even have encouraged experienced politicians to run). Formally, I hypothesize that increases in distributive spending or contingent liability awards, essentially any pork barreling, decreases the likelihood that an experienced challenger will run in the general election. As polarization increases, however, the effects of the pork barrel become consistent with the partisan expectations discussed throughout the first four chapters of this book. Specifically, increases in distributive spending will increase the likelihood of Republican incumbents' facing an experienced challenger and decrease the likelihood of this for Democratic incumbents. Conversely, increases in contingent liability awards will decrease the likelihood that Republican incumbents will face an experienced challenger and increase the likelihood that Democratic incumbents will.

Campaign Contributors as Rational Actors

The primary interest of this work as it relates to campaign spending is to show that polarization and the pork barrel affect the campaign spending of challengers and incumbents.[3] While the focus thus far has been on the candidates, the argument also makes several assumptions about the behavior of campaign donors worth presenting in more detail. Campaign donors are, first and foremost, strategic in their giving behavior, directing finite resources in ways meant to achieve their goals (Cann 2008; Lowry 2015; Romer and Snyder 1994; Stratmann 1992). The donation behavior of organized interests is perhaps the most studied in this area. While there is little support for the argument that interest groups are, in a general sense, able to directly affect the roll-call behavior of legislators with their campaign contributions (Ansolabehere, de Figueiredo, and Snyder 2003; Bronars and Lott 1997; Chappell 1982; Harden and Kirkland 2016; Wright 1985),[4] there is ample evidence that groups that contribute to campaigns have greater access to the legislators to whom they contribute (Austen-Smith 1995; Fouirnaies and Hall 2014; Kalla and Broockman 2016; Langbein 1986). Whether this giving behavior is directed toward gaining access (e.g., Wright 1990) or more simply supporting candidates and legislators who are like-minded from a policy perspective (Bronars and Lott 1997; Fox and Rothenberg 2011; Romer and Snyder 1994), policy concerns are clearly motivating these donations, suggesting a rational basis for giving.

Related to policy goals, there is a strong ideological component to campaign donations. Individual donors are found to be more politically sophisticated (Sorauf 1992), which implies that individual donors as a group exhibit stronger levels of partisanship and more extreme ideological identification and positions. Bonica (2013b, 2014) uses campaign donation data to place donors, groups, and candidates on an ideological continuum that correlates highly with common measures of legislator ideology (e.g., DW-NOMINATE). Just the fact that campaign contribution networks can be used in this fashion demonstrates that donors are rational in their behavior, correctly judging the policy positions of candidates and funneling resources to the candidates with whom they are most aligned. Campaign contributors are also strategic, in the sense that they consider the likely outcome of races in their decisions to donate. Lowry (2015), for example, finds that factors like timing and the competitiveness of races are better predictors of donation behavior than socioeconomic factors. Most groups have limited resources and seemingly prefer spending those resources where they will have the greatest impact on the outcome of elections. This is especially true of party committees and leadership political action committees, which are interested in building and maintaining majorities (Cann 2008; Currinder 2003).

The foregoing discussion serves to highlight that campaign contributors of all stripes are rational and strategic, motivated by policy goals best achieved by having one's preferred candidates win elections. Because challenging campaigns are inherently risky investments, donations to these campaigns, and therefore the resources challengers have available to spend, will increase in contexts that signal potential incumbent weakness. Examinations of the pork barrel and campaign finance are as uncommon as studies of the pork barrel and challenger quality. Lazarus, Glas, and Barbieri (2012) provide one quantitative analysis of this question. Looking only at incumbent receipts, they found that the campaign coffers of Democratic incumbents in 2008 increased with earmarks. Null results are reported for Democrats in 2010 and for Republicans in both years. Rocca and Gordon (2013) found a generally positive relationship between defense-related earmarks and contributions from political action committees active in that issue area. They do not, however, condition the effect of earmarks on the party of the member, including party only as a control variable.

Despite the general lack of quantitative work on the topic, my argument leads to several hypotheses regarding the pork barrel and campaign spending. In races featuring Republican incumbents, as polarization increases, I expect that increasing distributive spending will increase both challenger spending, because challengers are able to raise more money in this context, and incumbent spending, because incumbents are forced to spend more to shore up a potential electoral weakness. Similarly, increasing contingent liability awards will decrease both challenger and incumbent spending. On the other side of the partisan aisle, as polarization increases, increases in distributive spending are

Examining the dynamics of campaign fund-raising, Krasno, Green, and Cowden (1994) found that incumbents tend to raise money in response to challenger receipts, but challengers do not necessarily raise money in response to incumbent fund-raising activities. Simply, incumbents put more energy into fund-raising as the challenger raises more throughout the campaign. Challengers try to raise as much as they can regardless of the incumbent's fund-raising behavior. This, in combination with the findings in other work (Basinger and Ensley 2007; Green and Krasno 1988; Jacobson 1978), suggests potential endogeneity between some of the measures. Endogeneity between challenger experience and challenger spending, and between both of those variables and incumbent spending, was assessed through the estimation of two-stage least squares (2SLS) models. Given that the presence of an experienced challenger is dichotomous, it is instrumented using the method suggested by Wooldridge (2002, 621–623). The instrument is the predicted probability that the dichotomous variable equals 1, generated from the estimation of a probit model using all of the predictors from the second-stage regression and a set of variables, excluded from the second stage, as independent variables.[5] The natural log of lagged challenger contributions is used as an instrument for logged challenger spending. The natural log of lagged incumbent contributions, the natural log of district median income, and whether the incumbent ran in a contested primary are included, in part, for identification purposes in the incumbent spending model. All three are expected to increase spending. As reported in table 6.2 (later in this chapter), endogeneity bias exists in the incumbent spending, but not the challenger spending model. The F-test statistic in the challenger spending model equals 0.646 ($p = 0.436$). In the incumbent spending model, the F-test statistic equals 31.565 ($p < 0.001$). The adjustment of standard errors for clustering by election year and the inclusion of only one instrument per endogenous regressor preclude the estimation of instrument tests. The incumbent spending model was estimated, therefore, with unadjusted standard errors using the lagged log of challenger spending as an additional instrument so that a Sargan test could be estimated. The resulting χ^2 equals 0.147 ($p = 0.701$), suggesting the instruments are appropriate. The final models, presented in table 6.2, use ordinary least squares (OLS) for challenger spending and 2SLS for incumbent spending. In addition to all of the variables discussed in this paragraph, the challenger spending model includes the partisan normal vote, and both models include lagged incumbent vote share. Both models also include polarization, both measures of the pork barrel, an indicator for Democratic incumbents, and the interactions between polarization, Democratic incumbent, and each measure of pork. Finally, these models also control for the interactions between polarization, party, and ideological difference.

Challenger Experience Results

Table 6.1 presents the results of the challenger experience model for Democrats and Republicans. Several of the control variables have the expected effects on the emergence of an experienced challenger. Incumbents elected by larger margins in their last election, especially in districts for which partisanship is more favorable to the incumbent, are much less likely to face an experienced challenger. Standard deviation increases in the partisan normal vote and lagged incumbent vote share decrease the predicted probability of an experienced challenger running against a Democratic incumbent by 0.055 and 0.024, respectively. The corresponding decreases for Republican incumbents are 0.072 and 0.052. Freshmen from both parties are more likely to face an experienced challenger in their first reelection, with the predicted probability increasing 0.113 for Democratic incumbents and 0.031 for Republicans. Challenging Democratic incumbents is also affected by region and timing. Southern Democrats are less likely to face experienced challengers, while Democrats generally are more likely to face an experienced challenger just after redistricting.

Ideological distance significantly affects the likelihood of an experienced challenger, but in the opposite manner as was observed for primary competition. The existence of primary competition, as explained in chapter 5, decreases in likelihood with ideological extremity. Extremity, then, is a means of deterring competition from within the party. It also, however, serves to encourage experienced challengers from the other party to run. This finding is consistent with those of Canes-Wrone, Brady, and Cogan (2002), who found that incumbents suffer an

Table 6.1

Probit Estimates for the Likelihood of an Experienced Challenger

Variable	Democrats		Republicans	
	Coefficient	Std. Err.	Coefficient	Std. Err.
Polarization	0.908*	0.280	−0.327	0.341
Distributive spending	−0.158	0.113	−0.267*	0.066
x Polarization	0.163	0.214	0.248*	0.095
Contingent liability awards	0.146	0.097	0.084	0.147
x Polarization	−0.254	0.178	−0.171	0.201
Ideological difference	−0.098	0.753	−0.516	0.267
x Polarization	−1.009	1.195	1.178*	0.395
Normal vote	−2.819*	0.592	−3.086*	0.576
Lagged incumbent vote share	−0.795*	0.254	−1.598*	0.335
Freshman	0.436*	0.073	0.120†	0.063
Southern state	−0.221*	0.091	−0.027	0.072
Closed primary	0.124	0.111	0.091	0.070
Term limits	0.034	0.062	−0.053	0.092
Redistricting year	0.337*	0.168	0.006	0.073
Intercept	0.549	0.439	2.034*	0.461
Model statistics				
Observations	2,597		2,289	
Log Pseudolikelihood	−1,061.733		−1,042.632	
LR χ^2 (12)	274.321*		163.940*	
Percent correctly predicted	82.6%		80.8%	

Source: Author's analysis of original data and data from American National Election Studies (2007, 2011, 2015), Bonica (2013), Lewis et al. (2019), National Conference of State Legislatures (2015, 2018), U.S. Bureau of the Census (n.d.), and U.S. Bureau of Fiscal Service (2019).

* $p < 0.05$ (two-tailed test)

† $p < 0.05$ (one-tailed test, directional hypothesis expected)

Note: Standard errors are adjusted for clustering by election year.

electoral cost for extremity. General electorates, they explain, tend to prefer moderate candidates to extreme ones. Where extremity is perceived as a disadvantage for incumbents, potential challengers with electoral experience are more likely to run. Consistent with the primary competition model, these effects are only observed at higher levels of polarization. Figure 6.1 presents the marginal effects of ideological

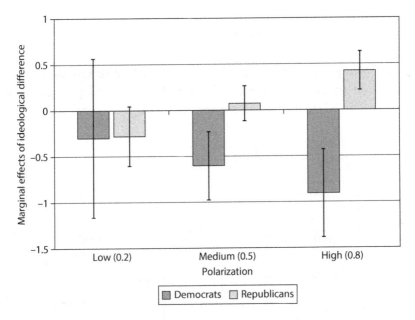

FIGURE 6.1 **Marginal effects of ideological difference on challenger experience**
The bars present the effect of a one-unit conservative increase in the ideological difference between legislators and their districts at three levels of polarization. Error bars represent 90 percent confidence intervals. *Source*: Author's analysis of original data and data from American National Election Studies (2007, 2011, 2015), Bonica (2013a), Lewis et al. (2019), National Conference of State Legislatures (2015, 2018), U.S. Bureau of the Census (n.d.), and U.S. Bureau of Fiscal Service (2019).

difference at low (0.2), medium (0.5), and high (0.8) levels of polarization. As the figure illustrates, the marginal effect of ideological distance, reflecting an increase in conservatism relative to the district, is significant and negative for Democrats starting from medium levels of polarization. A standard deviation increase in relative conservatism during medium polarization decreases the predicted probability of an experienced challenger running by 0.037. At high polarization, the decrease in probability is 0.072. The effect is significant and positive only at a high level of polarization for Republicans, where a standard deviation increase in conservatism increases the probability of facing an experienced challenger by 0.036.

The Deterrent Effects of the Pork Barrel

Figure 6.2a presents the marginal effects of distributive spending on the likelihood of an experienced challenger. The predicted probability of an experienced challenger across the range of distributive spending is

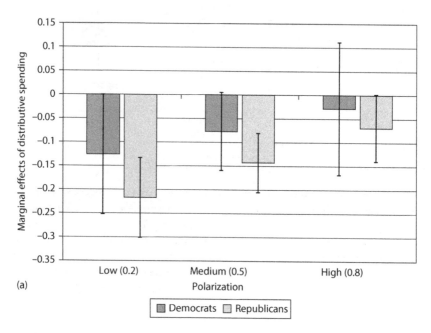

(a)

FIGURE 6.2 **Effects of distributive spending on challenger experience**
The bars in panel (a) present the effect of a one-unit increase in the congress-difference of logged real distributive spending at three levels of polarization. Error bars represent 90 percent confidence intervals. Curves in the panel (b) show the predicted probability of an experienced challenger across the range of differenced distributive spending under three conditions: against Democratic incumbents when polarization is low (equal to 0.2), against Republican incumbents when polarization is low (0.2), and against Republican incumbents at a medium level of polarization (0.5). Distributive spending, as depicted in panel (a), is significant in all three conditions. *Source*: Author's analysis of original data and data from American National Election Studies (2007, 2011, 2015), Bonica (2013a), Lewis et al. (2019), National Conference of State Legislatures (2015, 2018), U.S. Bureau of the Census (n.d.), and U.S. Bureau of Fiscal Service (2019).

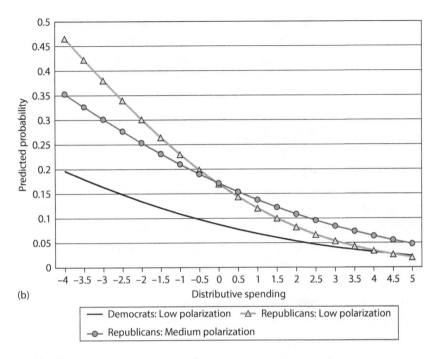

(b)

FIGURE 6.2 (*Continued*)

presented in figure 6.2b. Both panels show a significant deterrent effect of distributive spending except at high levels of polarization. Looking at figure 6.2a first, at low levels of polarization, experienced challengers are deterred from running against incumbents of both parties. Moving to medium levels of polarization, the effect is specific to Republican incumbents. At higher levels of polarization, the deterrent effect disappears. Predicted probabilities associated with the significant effects, low polarization for Democrats and low and medium polarization for Republicans, are presented in figure 6.2b. Predicted probabilities were generated holding variables besides distributive spending, polarization, and incumbent party identification at mean or base values for continuous and categorical variables, respectively. At low polarization, there are large decreases in the probability of an experienced challenger to incumbents of both parties moving across the range of distributive spending, although the decline is far more pronounced for Republican incumbents. The decrease is also very steep for Republican incumbents when polarization is at a medium level. In reality, very few districts see changes in distributive spending at the extreme values. Limiting the examination to the −1 to 1 range, which encompasses more than 95 percent of the observations, the deterrence effect is still sizable. For Democratic incumbents during low polarization, moving from −1 to 1 in the change in distributive spending decreases the predicted probability of facing an experienced challenger by 0.04, from 0.109 to 0.069. For Republicans, the decreases are 0.11 and 0.073 during low and medium polarization, respectively.

As discussed earlier in this chapter, experienced politicians are strategic actors and likely hold the same beliefs and make the same assumptions as those currently serving in Congress. The pork barrel is seen as electorally beneficial by state officials (Carey, Niemi, and Powell 1998; Ellickson and Whistler 2001; Thompson 1986). It makes sense that these same elected officials assume that a House incumbent who has brought federal money to the district is in a stronger electoral position. Interestingly, the deterrent effect fades at higher levels of polarization, suggesting that experienced politicians are not considering the distributive activities of incumbent members of House when deciding to run. While obtaining ideologically incongruous pork is not necessarily seen as a weakness, pork and the credit claiming that goes with it are certainly not considered incumbent strengths that would discourage experienced politicians from mounting a challenge. Relating the observed results to previous work, Bickers and Stein (1996), discussed earlier in this chapter, find a deterrent effect of the pork barrel in both primary and general elections, looking specifically at the emergence of experienced politicians. Their data are drawn from the 1990 election, a low-polarization context. By the measure employed here, polarization equals 0.26 in 1990, which is on the lower end of the scale. Consistent with their findings, both Democrats and Republicans in this study enjoy a significant deterrent effect from pork barreling at such a low level of polarization.

Campaign Spending Results

The challenger and incumbent spending model results are presented in table 6.2, the bottom of which contains the details of the aforementioned

Table 6.2

Results of the Challenger and Incumbent Spending Models

Variable	Challenger Spending (OLS)		Incumbent Spending (2SLS)	
	Coefficient	Std. Err.	Coefficient	Std. Err.
Democrat	−1.245	1.725	−0.024	0.134
Polarization	4.271	2.730	0.787*	0.329
x Democrat	2.080	3.658	−0.008	0.307
Distributive spending	0.303	0.290	0.161*	0.041
x Democrat	−0.245	0.451	−0.045	0.074
x Polarization	0.016	0.444	−0.136	0.083
x Democrat x Polarization	0.010	0.635	−0.093	0.106
Contingent liability awards	−0.439	0.364	−0.087	0.054
x Democrat	0.338	0.266	0.079	0.075
x Polarization	0.084	0.550	0.029	0.099
x Democrat x Polarization	0.155	0.355	−0.003	0.110
Ideological difference	1.846	2.016	0.503	0.319
x Democrat	−3.496	2.528	−0.662	0.427
x Polarization	−3.188	3.762	−0.983†	0.566
x Democrat x Polarization	4.242	4.300	1.173	0.760
Challenger experience	1.406*	0.167	1.092*	0.219
Challenger spending			−0.066^	0.018
Lagged challenger contributions	0.171*	0.027		
District median income			0.140*	0.058
Lagged incumbent contributions			0.759*	0.028
Contested primary			0.115*	0.017
Normal vote	−4.434*	0.940		
Lagged incumbent vote share	−8.777*	1.346	−0.647*	0.291
Intercept	14.670*	1.196	2.327*	0.735
Model statistics				
Observations	3,230		3,230	
Adjusted R^2	0.258		0.238	
Model χ^2	984.100*		231.720*	
Endogeneity F-test	0.646 (p = 0.436)		31.565 (p < 0.001)	
Sargan $\chi^2(1)$			0.147 (p = 0.701)	

Source: Author's analysis of original data and data from American National Election Studies (2007, 2011, 2015), Bonica (2013), Lewis et al. (2019), National Conference of State Legislatures (2015, 2018), U.S. Bureau of the Census (n.d.), and U.S. Bureau of Fiscal Service (2019).

* $p < 0.05$ (two-tailed)

† $p < 0.05$ (one-tailed, directional hypothesis expected)

^ $p < 0.05$ (two-tailed, coefficient opposite expectations)

Note: In both models, standard errors are adjusted for clustering by election year. The model χ^2 tests are the likelihood ratio test for the challenger spending model and the Wald test for the incumbent spending model. Overidentification tests for the validity of instruments are not available for cluster-adjusted standard errors. The Sargan test reported above is estimated on the model as presented with unadjusted standard errors.

endogeneity tests. The F-tests show endogeneity bias in the incumbent spending model but not the challenger spending model, and the Sargan test suggests that the instruments used for challenger experience and challenger spending are appropriate. Starting with ideological difference, campaign spending is the only set of outcomes in which differences between the incumbent and district largely have null effects. Ideological difference has no effect on incumbent spending and no effect on challenger spending against Republican incumbents. The only time ideological difference seems to matter is for challengers opposing Democratic incumbents when polarization is around a mid-level value. It is significant for values of polarization between 0.34 and 0.57 and has similar effects to those observed in the challenger experience model. An increase in Democratic incumbent conservatism relative to the district could be perceived as moderation, as opposed to extremity, and viewed as electorally advantageous. As a result, challengers spend less, presumably because they are less able to raise funds. At a polarization value of 0.48, an increase of one standard deviation in ideological difference (equal to 0.351) decreases challenger spending by 40 percent. Beyond ideology, having held elected office clearly enables challengers to spend more and forces incumbents to spend more in response to the emergence of a high-quality challenge. Experienced challengers spend 140.6 percent more than amateurs, and incumbents spend 109.2 percent more when facing an experienced challenger. Interestingly, controlling for challenger experience leads challenger spending to have a negative effect on incumbent spending, with a 1 percent increase in challenger spending causing a 0.066 percent decrease in incumbent spending. Green and Krasno (1988) suggest that the negative relationship between incumbent spending and electoral prosperity is the result of incumbents' spending more against high-quality challengers, who have the ability to raise and spend more. An interpretation of the results presented here, consistent with their findings, is that incumbents feel pressure to spend more against experienced challengers. Against amateurs, however, that pressure is reduced.[6]

The remaining control variables in both models have the expected effects. The log of lagged challenger contributions, which was used as an instrument for current challenger spending, has a positive effect. A 1 percent increase in logged challenger contributions increases current challenger spending by

0.171 percent. An increase of one standard deviation in the partisan normal vote, equal to 11.3 points, decreases challenger spending by 50.1 percent. Similarly, a one-point increase in lagged incumbent vote share decreases challenger spending by 8.777 percent, while an increase of one standard deviation in lagged incumbent vote share, equal to 15.4 points, effectively wipes out challenger spending. Lagged incumbent vote share, a sign of incumbent electoral safety, also has a negative effect on incumbent spending, with an increase of one standard deviation in lagged vote share causing a 10 percent decrease in incumbent spending. Finishing up the incumbent spending model, incumbents who raised more in their last election, possibly a sign of increased spending in the previous election, spend more in the current election, with spending increasing 0.759 percent for every 1 percent increase in lagged contributions. Echoing the discussion from the previous chapter, incumbents running in a contested primary spend more on their total campaign—an increase of 11.5 percent. Lastly, incumbents representing wealthier districts tend to spend more on their campaigns. A 1 percent increase in district median income leads to a 0.14 percent increase in incumbent spending.

The Pork Barrel and Campaign Spending

With respect to the conditioning effects of polarization, these are only observed for the effects of distributive spending on Democratic incumbent spending. Figure 6.3 presents the marginal effects of distributive spending across the range of polarization. Consistent with conditioning effects reported in other chapters, the effects of distributive spending are only significant at higher levels of polarization, starting from a value of 0.66. At a value of 0.68, roughly the level of polarization during the 2012 election, an increase of one standard deviation in the change in distributive spending decreases incumbent spending 2.2 percent. At a value of 0.8, roughly the level of polarization during the 2010 campaigns, the decrease in incumbent spending is 3.7 percent. Contingent liabilities do not affect Democratic incumbent spending, and neither pork barrel measure affects challenger spending against Democrats. Despite these null effects elsewhere, one can conclude that reduced

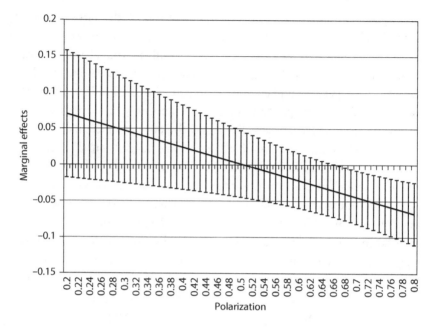

FIGURE 6.3 **Marginal effects of distributive spending on Democratic incumbent spending**
The curve presents the effect of a one-unit increase in the congress-difference of logged real distributive spending across the range of polarization. Error bars represent 90 percent confidence intervals. *Source*: Author's analysis of original data and data from American National Election Studies (2007, 2011, 2015), Bonica (2013a), Lewis et al. (2019), National Conference of State Legislatures (2015, 2018), U.S. Bureau of the Census (n.d.), and U.S. Bureau of Fiscal Service (2019).

incumbent spending reveals the perception, if not necessarily the reality, of increased electoral safety on the part of pork barreling Democrats when polarization is high.

A different pattern of results is found for Republican incumbents. Unlike for Democrats, both pork barrel measures affect the spending of both challengers and incumbents. Furthermore, the effects are nearly constant and almost always significant across the range of polarization. These effects are presented in figure 6.4. Looking first at figure 6.4a, which presents the marginal effects of both pork barrel measures on challenger spending against Republican incumbents, both measures change very little as polarization increases. The effects of both measures are in the predicted directions, positive for distributive spending and negative for contingent liabilities, and both are significant starting from a value of polarization of roughly 0.26. An increase of one standard deviation in the congress-difference in the log of distributive spending increases challenger spending by about 17 percent regardless of the level of polarization. Comparing this to the deterrent effect of distributive spending, campaign donors to the challenger may be seeing something that

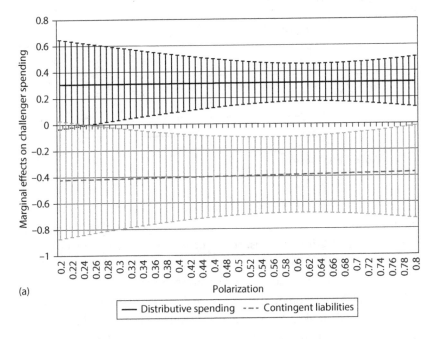

(a)

— Distributive spending   - - - Contingent liabilities

FIGURE 6.4 **Marginal effects of the pork barrel on campaign spending in Republican districts**

Both panels present the marginal effects of the congress-differences in the log of distributive spending and the log of contingent liability awards across the range of polarization. Panel (a) presents the effects on challenger spending; panel (b) presents the effects on incumbent spending. For all curves, error bars represent 90 percent confidence intervals. *Source*: Author's analysis of original data and data from American National Election Studies (2007, 2011, 2015), Bonica (2013a), Lewis et al. (2019), National Conference of State Legislatures (2015, 2018), U.S. Bureau of the Census (n.d.), and U.S. Bureau of Fiscal Service (2019).

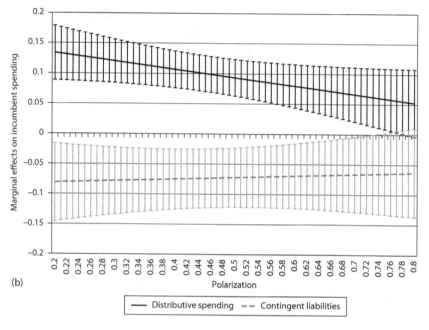

(b)

FIGURE 6.4 (*Continued*)

experienced politicians are not: Republican incumbents who secure substantial amounts of distributive spending have a potential weakness when
running for reelection. That is, these incumbents have pursued distributive activities that constituents might find unfavorable. I have argued that
this is particularly the case as polarization increases. This is the same
"observation" that potential primary challengers to Republican incumbents appear to make. An abundance of distributive spending can give
the appearance of an incumbent out of touch with the district, especially when polarization is high and constituents may be paying more
attention. The mirror image is found for contingent liability awards.
Rather than pork barreling leading to better-funded challengers, as was
the case for distributive spending, increases in conservative-friendly pork
are associated with decreasing challenger spending and, by assumption,
challengers with less funding. The marginal effect of contingent liability
awards varies slightly more with polarization than the marginal effect of
distributive spending does. Across the range of polarization, however,

the effect of a one-unit increase in the congress-difference in the log of contingent liability awards is around −0.4. This translates into a 39.7 percent decrease in challenger spending when contingent liability awards increase one standard deviation.

Figure 6.4b, showing the effects of the pork barrel on Republican incumbent spending, depicts a similar story. In this case, both pork barrel measures are significant across the range of polarization, except when polarization is at its highest levels (greater than 0.78 for distributive spending and greater than 0.73 for contingent liabilities). Another difference is seen for the effects of distributive spending, which vary more meaningfully across the range of polarization. Distributive spending has its largest effects at lower levels of polarization, with the effect decreasing as polarization increases. An increase of one standard deviation in distributive spending increases incumbent spending by as much as 7.3 percent (when polarization equals 0.2) and as little as 3 percent (when polarization equals 0.78). The same increase in contingent liabilities decreases incumbent spending by around 7 percent across the range of polarization. Considering incumbent spending a sign of electoral weakness, the same explanation offered previously in the discussion of challenger spending is appropriate here. Republican incumbents who secure large amounts of distributive spending find themselves spending more on their own campaigns. Securing large amounts of contingent liability awards places Republicans in a presumably safer position, leading to decreases in campaign spending. Even though the effects on incumbent spending are not significant at the highest levels of polarization, the results present clear evidence that the pork barrel matters for Republican incumbent spending. It matters when polarization is low and when it is relatively high.

Conclusion

Ultimately, most voters on Election Day are faced with a choice of two candidates. National forces are important. Views of the parties are important. Issues are important. These factors, however, affect voting and election outcomes only insofar as the candidates make them relevant to the electorate. When these forces are aligned against the incumbent, experienced politicians are encouraged to run and donors are encouraged to support the challenger's campaign. Experienced, well-funded challengers are then better able to capitalize on the presumed weaknesses of the incumbent. Conversely, an electoral context favoring the incumbent discourages the emergence of experienced challengers and leads to poorly funded challenging campaigns. Just as national forces and partisan conditions dictate the entry of experienced politicians and the amount of money challengers are able to spend, so too does the pork barrel. Experienced challengers spend more, and incumbents spend more when they face experienced challengers. Incumbents of both parties have the ability to procure distributive spending and deter the emergence of experienced challengers. As seen in previous chapters, however, incumbents need to be careful to secure pork consistent with the ideological leanings of their constituents. Pork barreling Democrats see no changes in the spending of their electoral challengers, but Republicans do. Too much distributive spending or too few contingent liability awards lead to better-funded Democratic challengers and the need for increases in their own campaign spending. Conversely, Democratic incumbents who increase distributive spending in their districts, particularly during periods of higher polarization, spend less on their campaigns.

The high-polarization case is an interesting one. This is where I argue one should observe the strongest ideologically consistent effects of the pork barrel on election outcomes. At higher levels of polarization, there are no indirect effects of the pork barrel on campaign spending in Democratic districts. The deterrent effect disappears and, as seen in chapter 4, there are no effects of the pork barrel on primary competition against Democratic incumbents either. The only effect that remains for Democrats is a decrease in incumbent spending as distributive spending increases, suggesting that pork barreling Democrats feel less pressure to spend on their campaigns. This could be due to an increase in popularity among constituents similar to what is observed in Stein and Bickers (1994a). For Republican incumbents, the deterrent effect in the general elections similarly disappears. Making matters worse, Republican incumbents who increase distributive spending find themselves more likely to face a primary challenger. If a primary challenger emerges, incumbents spend 11.5 percent more than if they run unopposed in the primary. The conclusion that challengers who spend more perform better in elections is uncontested in the literature. There has been, as discussed earlier, some debate over the effects of incumbent spending. I have followed the reasoning that incumbent spending is an indicator of electoral weakness; incumbents spend more on their campaigns only when they feel they must. On this point, the results presented in chapter 4 show that voters become less likely to vote for the incumbent when incumbent spending increases. Voters generally, then, are more likely to vote for Democrats who secure more distributive spending and Republicans who secure more contingent liability awards (and therefore spend less on their campaigns). Voters are also less likely to vote for Republicans who secure more distributive spending (and spend more on their campaigns as a result). Intermediate outcomes such as the emergence of an experienced challenger are also important. Where the pork barrel affects these intermediate outcomes, there are also indirect effects of the pork barrel on ultimate outcomes—on votes, as just discussed, and on vote share, which is the focus of the next chapter.

7

Election Outcomes

ON ELECTION DAY 2006, the Democrats gained thirty-one seats in the House of Representatives and six seats in the Senate, giving them a majority in both houses of Congress. While such gains for the out-party are common in midterm elections, the rationale offered by Republican elites and conservative commentators is worth noting. The major story woven throughout the election coverage was the war in Iraq. Democrats had a solid issue with which they could energize their base and win over Independents in the electorate. Scandal too had dealt a blow to the Republican Party. In the days that followed, however, conservatives started attributing Republican losses to their abandonment of limited government, particularly in the realm of spending. In a speech delivered at the National Lawyers Convention of the Federalist Society on November 16, 2006, Senator John McCain offered the following: "We were elected to reduce the size of government and enlarge the sphere of free and private initiative. We increased the size of government in the false hope that we could bribe the public into keeping us in office" (McCain 2006). These sentiments were expressed in several columns discussing Republican losses (e.g., George Will's column in the November 9 *Washington Post* and Pat Toomey's in the November 10 *National Review Online*). With respect to academic investigations, Panagopoulos and Schank (2008) provide an excellent account of how pork barreling in the 2005 transportation funding authorization, SAFETEA-LU

(PL 109–59), may have contributed to Republican losses in the 2006 elections. Were Republicans unwilling to admit the plummeting popularity of the war and ignoring the taint of scandal, or is there something to the argument that Republicans abandoned their small-government principles? The mass public, at least, seemed to have bought the argument. In a poll conducted November 9 and 10 by Princeton Survey Research Associates International and *Newsweek*, 67 percent of respondents said Republican handling of spending and the deficit was a major reason for the Democrats' success. Only 8 percent said it was not a reason at all.

Assuming Senator McCain's assessment of spending is correct, the previous chapters suggest reasons why spendthrift Republicans, at least in the sphere of distributive politics, may have suffered at the polls. By the measure used here, polarization in 2006 was not yet high enough for distributive spending to affect primary competition. Republican incumbents, however, would be facing a greatly reduced deterrent effect against experienced general-election challengers as well as challengers that were better funded. Distributive politics were far from the most important cause of Republican losses in 2006. Yet, with polarization on the rise, Republicans bore electoral costs for their distributive activities. As election outcomes are *the* outcomes of interest in both a practical and an academic sense, this chapter represents the culmination of the district-level analyses presented in the two previous chapters. As in previous chapters, I will once again demonstrate that the direct effects of the pork barrel are conditioned by polarization. This chapter also brings together the district-level analyses in another way. The foci of those analyses—contested primaries, challenger experience, and fund-raising—are argued to affect House election outcomes. As the pork barrel and polarization affect those variables, they work through them to indirectly affect electoral outcomes. Ample attention, therefore, will be paid to the total effects of the pork barrel, both direct and indirect, on the electoral fortunes of incumbents.

The Pork Barrel and the Electoral Connection

Mayhew's suggestion that pork is an important source of credit claiming, added to observations of universalism, has led to theoretical arguments supporting the assumption that voters generally prefer particularistic benefits and reward legislators who secure those benefits (Niou and Ordeshook 1985; Shepsle and Weingast 1981; Weingast, Shepsle, and Johnsen 1981). The assumption of electoral benefits finds justification in work finding that electorally vulnerable legislators tend to secure a larger share of spending (Lazarus 2009; Stein and Bickers 1994a) and in work observing that party leaders use pork to promote policy and electoral ends (Cann and Sidman 2011; Evans 1994, 2004). Previous chapters paid ample attention to research at the individual level and to the effects of pork as they work through district-level factors. Summarizing that literature, most scholars assume this positive relationship between pork and the likelihood of voting for the incumbent (e.g., Stein and Bickers 1994a), but such a general relationship has been difficult to verify empirically (Johannes and McAdams 1981) or may be conditioned by individual-level factors such as ideology (Kriner and Reeves 2012). The assumption of electoral benefits from pork barreling informs district-level models reporting a deterrent effect with respect to experienced challengers (Bickers and Stein 1996; Lazarus, Glas, and Barbieri 2012) and increases in campaign contributions to the incumbent (Lazarus, Glas, and Barbieri 2012; Rocca and Gordon 2013).

Despite the straightforward logic of linking universalism to the electoral connection, several works cast doubt on the implications of the theoretical models. Stein and Bickers (1994b), for example, note that actual distributions of pork are not necessarily universal and the assumption of voter knowledge, essential for an electoral connection, is unrealistic. Party emerges in the literature as a major factor influencing the distribution of benefits. The previously cited work by Bickers and Stein (2000) finds a relative increase in funding for contingent liabilities coinciding with Republicans' regaining the majority in both chambers subsequent to the 1994 elections. Several scholars (Engstrom and Vanberg 2010; Lazarus and Steigerwalt 2009; Levitt and Snyder 1995) have observed that Democrats tend to receive more funding than Republicans from direct payment and grant programs and earmarks. Other works have noted more general partisan effects. Berry, Burden, and Howell (2010a) conclude that the life span and funding of distributive programs depend on the strength, measured in seat shares, of the party that enacted the program. Considering funding of specific types of pork, Balla et al. (2002) find a majority-party bias in the value of higher education earmarks received by members of Congress. Similarly, Carsey and Rundquist (1999) find stronger support for a party-centered explanation for the distribution of military pork than for a committee-centered explanation. Recognizing the role of the executive branch in administering these programs, Bertelli and Grose (2009) find that federal funding of Department of Labor and Department of Defense programs tends to go to states represented by senators who are ideologically proximate to those respective Cabinet secretaries. Although ideological proximity is different from party congruence, one could reasonably assume that copartisans are, on average, closer to one another.

Partisan differences in the distribution of benefits, especially where those differences identify a Democratic or Republican preference for particular types of pork, inform the observed partisan differences in the electoral effects of the pork barrel. Alvarez and Saving (1997) and Lazarus and Reilly (2010) report a positive relationship between pork and Democratic vote shares, with null effects for Republicans. Sellers (1997) reaches a similar conclusion on the basis of fiscal liberalism, whereby liberals benefit electorally from pork and conservatives do not. Lazarus and Reilly (2010) present more detailed analyses with respect to types of programs, showing that Democrats benefit from more traditional pork barrel spending (e.g., direct payment and grant programs) while Republicans in conservative districts tend to benefit from contingent liabilities. Looking at presidential elections, Kriner and Reeves (2012, 2015) find a positive relationship between federal grant spending and county-level vote share that increases in strength as the county liberalism increases. In most of the research analyzing election outcomes, and in some of the research considering the distribution of pork, an ideological basis for partisan differences is suggested. No work, however, contemplates a role for polarization in activating these latent ideological preferences. This might be a consequence of null findings overall at the district level (e.g., Feldman and Jondrow 1984), null findings specifically for Republicans (e.g., Alvarez and Saving 1997), or positive relationships for which conditioning by partisanship or ideology is not considered (Levitt and Snyder 1997; Stratmann 2013). The previous chapters have presented arguments and evidence supporting an ideological basis for different partisan effects of the pork barrel and for the role of polarization in conditioning these effects. These arguments are brought to bear in the present analysis of House election outcomes.

The foregoing discussion and especially the historical discussion and the results of the individual-level analyses lead to several expectations for the relationship between polarization, distributive benefits, and electoral outcomes in the House. First, as polarization increases, the effect of distributive spending should become increasingly positive for Democrats (i.e., the interaction between polarization and distributive spending will carry a positive coefficient for Democratic incumbents). For Republicans, the effects of distributive spending will become increasingly negative as polarization increases (i.e., the interaction will have a negative coefficient). Opposite effects should be observed for contingent liability programs. As polarization grows, increases in contingent liabilities will provide larger electoral benefits to Republican incumbents and larger electoral costs to Democratic incumbents. Put another way, the coefficients on the interaction between polarization and contingent liabilities will be positive for Republicans and negative for Democrats. In addition to these direct effects, the pork barrel is expected to have indirect effects on election outcomes through the variables considered in previous chapters. Specifically, Republican incumbents will be further harmed by distributive spending when polarization is high because of the increased likelihood of running in a contested primary. Starting from moderate levels of polarization, Republicans are expected to face an additional cost from distributive spending, and receive an additional benefit from contingent liability awards, through increases and decreases in challenger spending from those different sources of pork, respectively. The same costs from distributive spending and benefits from contingent liabilities may also work through respective increases and decreases in incumbent spending at low through moderate levels of polarization. For Democratic incumbents, I expect to observe additional electoral benefits of distributive spending working though decreases in incumbent spending when polarization is high. Incumbents of both parties will also enjoy a deterrent effect with respect to challenger experience in the general election as distributive spending increases; this deterrent effect is present, however, only at lower levels of polarization.

Data and Methods

The unit of analysis is the House district, and the dependent variable is the incumbent's share of the two-party vote. Consistent with prior work on House elections (Basinger and Ensley 2007; Green and Krasno 1988; Jacobson 1978), incumbent vote share is estimated via two-stage least squares (2SLS). To account for the endogeneity of particular variables related to election outcomes, the following variables are included as endogenous regressors: whether the incumbent ran in a contested primary (coded 1 for contested primaries, 0 if the incumbent ran unopposed); challenger experience (coded 1 if the challenger held elected office, 0 otherwise); the natural log of challenger spending; and the natural log of incumbent spending. As described in chapters 5 and 6, the pork barrel and polarization affect each of these variables. Their inclusion in the 2SLS model of incumbent vote share, as noted in the introduction to this chapter, allows for a full discussion of the direct and indirect effects of pork and polarization on vote share. Contested primary election and challenger experience are both dichotomous. To instrument for these variables, I use the method suggested by Wooldridge (2002, 621–633) and introduced in the previous chapter.[1] The lagged natural log of challenger contributions and of incumbent contributions, as well as the natural log of district median income, are included as instruments for challenger and incumbent spending. Post-estimation diagnostic testing suggests that there is indeed endogeneity and the instruments are valid.[2] Similar to the previous district-level analyses, incumbent vote share is modeled as a function of distributive spending, contingent liability awards, and their interactions with polarization and incumbent party.

The model controls for the ideological difference between the incumbent and the district and its interactions with incumbent party and polarization. Ideological difference is expected to have effects on vote share similar to what was observed in the analysis of challenger experience. Increasing conservatism is assumed to be a move toward extremity for Republicans and leads to an increased likelihood that the challenger is experienced. Increasing conservatism is assumed to be a move toward moderation for Democrats, resulting in a decreased likelihood that the challenger is experienced. These results, consistent with the findings of Canes-Wrone, Brady, and Cogan (2002) regarding ideological extremity, are expected to carry through to the general election with increasing conservatism relative to the district leading to lower vote shares for Republicans and higher vote shares for Democrats. Again, these effects should increase in strength as polarization increases. Incumbent vote share is also expected to be affected by the district normal vote, the incumbent's vote share in the last election (both with positive effects), whether it is a midterm election year, the president's Gallup approval rating in October of the election year, and the percent change in real gross domestic product for the election year. The last three variables are interacted with an indicator of whether the incumbent is a member of the president's party, expecting the effects to be negative, positive, and positive, respectively, for the president's copartisans.

District-Level Results

The results of the 2SLS estimation of incumbent vote share are presented in table 7.1. As noted earlier, postestimation testing revealed significant endogeneity bias and suggested that the instruments used for the endogenous variables are appropriate. The control variables largely affect incumbent vote share as expected. An increase of one standard deviation in the partisan normal vote increases incumbent vote share by 2.9 points. Likewise, an increase of one standard deviation in lagged incumbent vote share increases current vote share by five points. Naturally, the safest incumbents are those who have performed well electorally in the past and whose district partisanship strongly favors their party. During midterm elections, incumbents from the president's party can expect their vote share to be five-and-a-half points lower, on average, while incumbents of the opposition party can expect an increase of 1.7 points in their vote share. Members of the president's party benefit from the popular approval of the president, gaining 3.4 points in their vote share for an increase of one standard deviation in approval. Interestingly, after controlling for presidential approval and midterm effects, all incumbents benefit from economic improvement.

Table 7.1

Two-Stage Least Squares Model of Incumbent Vote Share

Variables	Coefficient	Std. Err.
Democrat	0.043	0.034
Polarization	0.026	0.048
x Democrat	−0.065	0.065
Distributive spending	−0.003	0.006
x Democrat	−0.024	0.016
x Polarization	−0.009	0.010
x Democrat x Polarization	0.057*	0.024
Contingent liability awards	−0.003	0.010
x Democrat	−0.003	0.013
x Polarization	0.022	0.015
x Democrat x Polarization	−0.021	0.020
Ideological difference	0.007	0.022
x Democrat	−0.055	0.036
x Polarization	−0.085	0.059
x Democrat x Polarization	0.296*	0.112
Contested primary	−0.042*	0.020
Challenger experience	−0.082*	0.032
ln(Challenger spending)	−0.003†	0.002
ln(Incumbent spending)	0.000	0.004
Normal vote	0.259*	0.031
Lagged incumbent vote share	0.322*	0.050
President's party	−0.073	0.044
Midterm	0.017†	0.009
x President's party	−0.055*	0.013
October presidential approval	−0.001	0.001
x President's party	0.003*	0.001
% Change in RGDP	0.012*	0.006
x President's party	−0.019	0.010
Intercept	0.341*	0.102
Model statistics		
Observations	3,221	
Adjusted R^2	0.497	
Wald $\chi^2(28)$	719.492*	
Endogeneity $F(4,13)$	11.713 ($p < 0.001$)	
Sargan $\chi^2(1)$	0.461 ($p = 0.497$)	

Source: Author's analysis of original data and data from American National Election Studies (2007, 2011, 2015), Bonica (2013), Lewis et al. (2019), Roper Center for Public Opinion Research (2019), U.S. Bureau of the Census (n.d.), U.S. Bureau of Economic Analysis (2018), and U.S. Bureau of Fiscal Service (2019).

* $p < 0.05$ (two-tailed test)

† $p < 0.05$ (one-tailed test, directional hypothesis expected)

Note: Standard errors are adjusted for clustering by election year. Overidentification tests for the validity of instruments are not available for cluster-adjusted standard errors. The Sargan test reported here is estimated on the model as presented with unadjusted standard errors.

An increase of one standard deviation in the annual change in RGDP increases the vote share of all incumbents by 2.5 points.

Rounding out discussion of the control variables, ideological difference relates to incumbent vote share in a manner similar to what Canes-Wrone, Brady, and Cogan (2002) report. Ideological difference is only significant at higher levels of polarization, as alluded to in the introduction and presented in figure 7.1. The negative coefficient for the ideological difference-polarization interaction and the positive coefficient for the three-way interaction that includes the incumbent's party identification suggest that incumbents are punished for ideological extremity relative

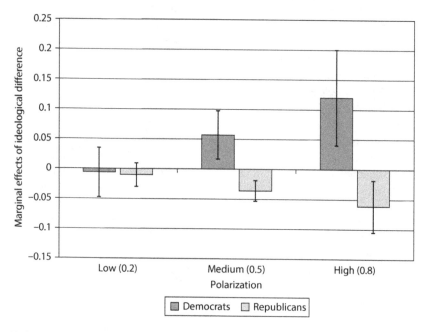

FIGURE 7.1 **Marginal effects of ideological difference on vote share**
Bars represent the marginal effect of a one-unit conservative increase in ideological difference at low, medium, and high levels of polarization in the partisan public. Error bars represent 90 percent confidence intervals. *Source*: Author's analysis of original data and data from American National Election Studies (2007, 2011, 2015), Bonica (2013a), Lewis et al. (2019), Roper Center for Public Opinion Research (2019), U.S. Bureau of the Census (n.d.), U.S. Bureau of Economic Analysis (2018), and U.S. Bureau of Fiscal Service (2019).

to the district. The measure in this analysis is not extremity per se. The results, however, are substantively related to those of Canes-Wrone, Brady, and Cogan (2002) if we make the safe assumption that an increase in conservatism represents a move toward moderation for Democratic incumbents and a move towards extremity for Republican incumbents. Specifically, when polarization is at a medium level—equal to 0.5, for example—a one-standard-deviation conservative increase in ideological difference increases Democratic vote share by two points. When polarization is high, equal to 0.8, the same conservative increase boosts Democratic vote share by 4.2 points. At medium and high levels of polarization, the same conservative increase decreases Republican vote share by 1.3 points and 2.2 points, respectively. The incentive to moderate, however, is balanced by the potential cost of moderation working through contested primaries. As reported in chapter 5, starting from moderate levels of polarization (0.38 for Democrats and 0.51 for Republicans), increasing conservatism increases the likelihood of a contested primary for Democrats and decreases it for Republicans. Although moderation provides a direct benefit to vote share, if it leads to a contested primary, incumbents can expect to pay a cost of 4.2 points, more than negating the direct benefits of moderation.

Direct Effects of the Pork Barrel on Incumbent Vote Share

Figures 7.2 and 7.3 depict the effects of one-unit increases in distributive spending and contingent liability awards, respectively, on incumbent vote share. As in previous chapters, effects are presented for low (0.2), medium (0.5), and high (0.8) levels of polarization. Error bars represent 90 percent confidence intervals, except for Democrats during low and medium polarization in figure 7.2. Those estimated effects are opposite expectations, making 95 percent confidence intervals more appropriate. Considering Democrats and distributive spending first, the expected growth of the marginal effect coinciding with increasing polarization is present. Also as expected, the effects of distributive spending are not significant until polarization reaches relatively high levels. At these

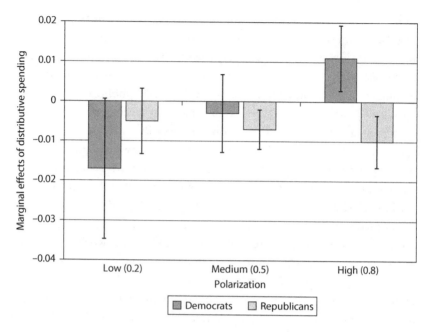

FIGURE 7.2 Marginal effects of distributive spending on vote share
Bars represent the marginal effect of a one-unit increase in the change in the natural log of distributive spending in the district at low, medium, and high levels of polarization in the partisan public. Error bars represent 90 percent confidence intervals, except for Democrats during low and medium polarization. Since these marginal effects are the opposite of expectations, the stricter 95 percent confidence intervals are presented, signifying two-tailed tests of significance. *Source*: Author's analysis of original data and data from American National Election Studies (2007, 2011, 2015), Bonica (2013a), Lewis et al. (2019), Roper Center for Public Opinion Research (2019), U.S. Bureau of the Census (n.d.), U.S. Bureau of Economic Analysis (2018), and U.S. Bureau of Fiscal Service (2019).

higher levels of polarization, the effect is positive and significant, with an increase of one standard deviation in distributive spending adding six-tenths of a point to incumbent vote share. The effects for Republican incumbents strongly conform to expectations. The effect of distributive spending is always negative, and its magnitude marginally increases with polarization. Effects are significant at moderate and higher levels of polarization, but not at lower levels. At medium and high levels of

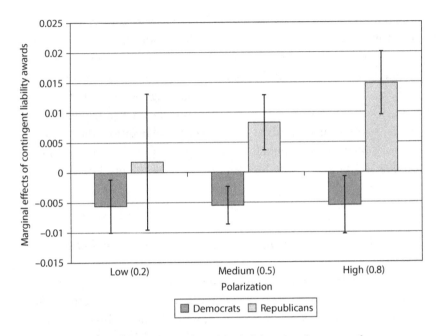

FIGURE 7.3 **Marginal effects of contingent liability awards on vote share**
Bars represent the marginal effect of a one-unit increase in the change in the natural log of contingent liability awards in the district at low, medium, and high levels of polarization in the partisan public. Error bars represent 90 percent confidence intervals. *Source*: Author's analysis of original data and data from American National Election Studies (2007, 2011, 2015), Bonica (2013a), Lewis et al. (2019), Roper Center for Public Opinion Research (2019), U.S. Bureau of the Census (n.d.), U.S. Bureau of Economic Analysis (2018), and U.S. Bureau of Fiscal Service (2019).

polarization, an increase of one standard deviation in distributive spending is expected to decrease the vote share of Republican incumbents by four-tenths of a point and five-tenths of a point, respectively.

A slightly different story emerges in figure 7.3, but one that still supports the argument that the pork barrel is an ideological issue. For Democratic incumbents, the effect of contingent liability awards is negative, significant, and nearly constant across the range of polarization. An increase of one standard deviation in contingent liability awards decreases vote share between five-tenths and six-tenths of a point. The effects for Republican incumbents are the mirror image of those observed for distributive spending. The effect of contingent liability awards is always positive, grows in magnitude with increasing polarization, and is significant at medium and higher, but not lower, levels of polarization. An increase of one standard deviation in contingent liability awards increases vote share by 0.8 and 1.5 points at medium and high levels of polarization, respectively. While Democrats tend to be punished for pursuing loan and insurance programs regardless of the level of polarization, the now familiar story emerges for Republicans. This type of pork benefits incumbents as expected, but voters do not seem to pay attention until polarization is high enough.

Indirect and Total Effects of Pork on Vote Share

Up to this point, the narrative has tended to focus more on what happens to Republican incumbents. The discussion of the indirect effects of pork barreling is no different. Practically no indirect effects are observed for Democratic incumbents, discussed in a later paragraph. For Republicans, the results reported in previous chapters all come to bear on the relationship between pork and general election vote share. Pork directly affects Republican vote share, but also influences primary contestation, challenger experience, and challenger spending, all of which also significantly affect vote share. All of the remaining figures in this chapter, except figure 7.7, are presented as flowcharts depicting the different ways pork affects vote share and include calculations of the total effect of an increase of one standard deviation in the relevant pork barrel measure.

The low-polarization case (figure 7.4) is a good place to start and the easiest to explain. It also demonstrates the conditions under which Republicans electorally benefit from distributive spending. At low levels of polarization, distributive spending affects vote share only through challenger experience. Figure 7.2 shows that the direct effect is not significant. Likewise, distributive spending does not directly affect primary contestation (chapter 5) or challenger spending (chapter 6). Chapter 6 detailed the deterrent effects of distributive spending at low and medium levels of polarization. These are the effects that matter here. Increasing distributive

Low polarization

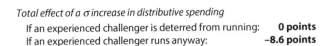

Total effect of a σ increase in distributive spending
If an experienced challenger is deterred from running: **0 points**
If an experienced challenger runs anyway: **-8.6 points**

FIGURE 7.4 **Effects of distributive spending on Republican vote share during low polarization**
The minus sign leading from distributive spending to challenger experience signifies the negative relationship between spending and the likelihood that the challenger has electoral experience. Numbers associated with arrows in the flowchart identify the direction and magnitude of the effects. For example, if an experienced challenger runs, the expected increase in the natural log of challenger spending is 1.406. This increase in challenger spending is expected to decrease incumbent vote share by 0.004 (four-tenths of a point). The effect (−0.004) is the product of the change in challenger spending resulting from the presence of an experienced challenger (1.406) and the coefficient on challenger spending in the vote share model (−0.003). Challenger experience also carries a direct effect on vote share of −0.082, or −8.2 points. *Source*: Author's analysis of original data and data from American National Election Studies (2007, 2011, 2015), Bonica (2013a), Lewis et al. (2019), Roper Center for Public Opinion Research (2019), U.S. Bureau of the Census (n.d.), U.S. Bureau of Economic Analysis (2018), and U.S. Bureau of Fiscal Service (2019).

spending decreases the likelihood of an experienced challenger's running. Challenger experience has a direct effect of −8.2 points on vote share. Working through increased challenger spending, challenger experience further reduces incumbent vote share another four-tenths of a point, for a total cost of 8.6 points. When polarization is low, Republican incumbents have an incentive to secure distributive spending. There is no direct cost for this type of pork barreling, and the deterrent effect on experienced challengers means potentially avoiding a heavy electoral cost of 8.6 points.

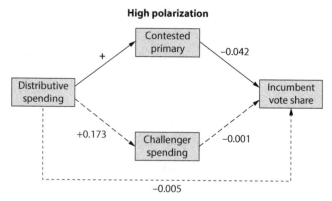

High polarization

Total effect of a σ increase in distributive spending
If a challenger runs in the primary: **−4.8 points**
If the primary is unopposed: **−0.6 points**

FIGURE 7.5 Effects of distributive spending on Republican vote share during high polarization
The three sets of arrows depict the direct effect of distributive spending on incumbent vote share and the indirect effects of distributive spending working through primaries and general-election challenger spending. The plus sign linking distributive spending to contested primaries signifies the positive relationship between distributive spending and the likelihood that the primary election is contested. As in the previous figure, the numbers associated with arrows identify the effects stemming from an increase of one standard deviation in distributive spending. *Source*: Author's analysis of original data and data from American National Election Studies (2007, 2011, 2015), Bonica (2013a), Lewis et al. (2019), Roper Center for Public Opinion Research (2019), U.S. Bureau of the Census (n.d.), U.S. Bureau of Economic Analysis (2018), and U.S. Bureau of Fiscal Service (2019).

The high polarization context is depicted in figure 7.5. Not unlike the low polarization case, the conclusion here is straightforward: Republican incumbents should not push to increase distributive spending in their districts. Unlike under low polarization, distributive spending in the high-polarization context has direct effects on vote share and indirect effects through primaries and challenger spending, but not challenger experience. Whereas the emphasis during periods of low polarization is on the deterrent effect, pork barreling enough to deter an experienced challenger from emerging, the emphasis during high polarization is on the encouragement, or antideterrent, effect in primaries. The direct effect of distributive spending is a decrease of five-tenths of a point when distributive spending increases by one standard deviation. Distributive spending also has two indirect effects when polarization is high. First, increases in spending increase the likelihood that the incumbent will be challenged in the primary. As the literature on primary elections makes clear, being defeated in the primary is exceptionally rare, but there is a significant cost to facing a challenge nonetheless. In table 7.1, that cost is estimated as 4.2 points. Second, increases in distributive spending are also associated with increases in challenger spending. An increase of one standard deviation in distributive spending increases the natural log of challenger spending by 0.173, which in turn decreases vote share by one-tenth of a point. If the incumbent is fortunate enough to avoid a primary challenge, the net effect on vote share is a decrease of six-tenths of a point. If the increase in distributive spending is enough to trigger the encouragement effect, the net decrease in vote share is 4.8 points. Either way, boosting distributive spending is costly for Republican incumbents.

When polarization is near the middle of its range, the situation confronting Republicans appears more complex. As figures 7.6 and 7.7 demonstrate, however, complexity of the context is not necessarily complexity of the conclusion, which is the same as when polarization is high: Republican incumbents are harmed electorally by distributive spending. The context is complicated because distributive spending exerts countervailing forces on vote share. This differs from the low and high polarization cases, under which the direct and indirect effects point in a consistent direction, or no direction at all for direct effects when polarization is low. As pictured in figure 7.6, distributive spending has negative direct effects on vote share and negative indirect effects through challenger spending. The depressive effect on vote share is balanced by the deterrent effect on experienced challengers. As the figure makes clear, however, whether an experienced challenger is deterred from running or not, the net effect of an increase in distributive spending on vote share is negative. Considering the familiar increase of one standard deviation in distributive spending, the direct effect is a decrease in incumbent vote share of four-tenths of a point. The log of challenger spending is expected to increase 0.17, contributing an additional cost of one-tenth of a point, for a net effect

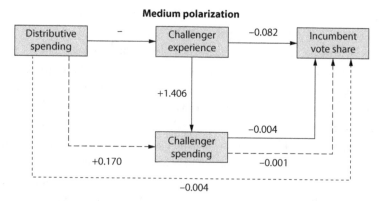

Medium polarization

Total effect of a σ increase in distributive spending
If an experienced challenger is deterred from running: **−0.5 points**
If an experienced challenger runs anyway: **−9.1 points**

FIGURE 7.6 **Effects of distributive spending on Republican vote share during medium polarization**
Three sets of arrows are depicted here. The solid arrows relate to the effect of distributive spending working through challenger experience. The dashed arrows represent the effect of an increase in distributive spending directly through challenger spending (i.e., not through challenger experience first). The dotted arrow shows the direct effect of an increase in distributive spending on vote share. *Source*: Author's analysis of original data and data from American National Election Studies (2007, 2011, 2015), Bonica (2013a), Lewis et al. (2019), Roper Center for Public Opinion Research (2019), U.S. Bureau of the Census (n.d.), U.S. Bureau of Economic Analysis (2018), and U.S. Bureau of Fiscal Service (2019).

of −0.005, or a decrease of half of a point. If the increase in distributive spending is enough to deter the entry of an experienced challenger, already an unlikely occurrence, this is the total effect of increasing distributive spending. If an experienced challenger does run, the indirect cost of 8.6 points, working through challenger experience and challenger spending, is added for a total decrease in vote share of 9.1 points. The deterrence effect and expected effects of distributive spending on vote share are presented in greater detail in figure 7.7.

Figure 7.7a shows the predicted probability of an experienced challenger's running, across the range of the congress-difference in the natural log of real distributive spending. In an effort to find any net positive effects

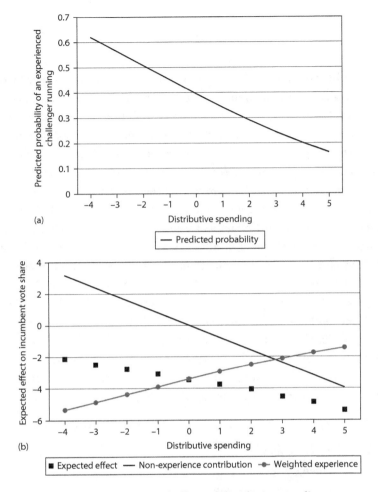

FIGURE 7.7 Deterrent and expected effects of distributive spending
Panel (a) presents the predicted probability of an experienced challenger's running during periods of medium polarization for freshman Republican incumbents. The partisan normal vote and lagged incumbent vote share are held at one standard deviation below the mean, and all other variables from the challenger experience model presented in chapter 6 are held at their mean or median values for continuous and categorical variables, respectively. Panel (b) presents the expected effect of distributive spending on incumbent vote share. The expected effect is calculated as the sum of the following:

1. The direct effect of distributive spending (DS) on vote share: $-0.007 \times DS$
2. The indirect effect of spending through challenger spending: $0.311 \times -0.003 \times DS$ (note that the sum of 1 and 2 produces the "Non-Experience Contribution" line)
3. The indirect effect through challenger experience: -0.086, which includes the direct effect of challenger experience (-0.082) and its effect through increased challenger spending (-0.004), multiplied by the predicted probability of an experienced challenger's running, as presented in the left panel (the light gray line with circular markers)

Source: Author's analysis of original data and data from American National Election Studies (2007, 2011, 2015), Bonica (2013a), Lewis et al. (2019), Roper Center for Public Opinion Research (2019), U.S. Bureau of the Census (n.d.), U.S. Bureau of Economic Analysis (2018), and U.S. Bureau of Fiscal Service (2019).

for distributive spending, I stacked the deck in favor of deterrence by considering a context that should produce a greater likelihood of an experienced challenger's running.[3] Predicted probabilities are calculated using the estimates presented in the right panel of table 6.1 for freshman Republicans at a medium (0.5) level of polarization, holding the partisan normal vote and lagged incumbent vote share at one standard deviation below the mean. All other variables are held at their mean or median values for continuous and categorical variables, respectively. Figure 7.7b depicts the expected total effects on incumbent vote share, similar to what is presented in figure 7.6 with a couple of adjustments. First, rather than an increase of one standard deviation, changes in distributive spending run across its range. Second, the indirect effect of challenger experience is included as a weighted effect; it is the total indirect effect of −0.086 multiplied by the predicted probability that an experienced challenger runs. The expected effect, depicted as square black points, is the sum of the nonexperience contribution and weighted experience and is calculated as follows, where *DS* stands for distributive spending and P_{CE} stands for the predicted probability of an experienced challenger's running:

$$Expected\ Effect = (-0.007 \times DS) + (0.311 \times -0.003 \times DS) + (-0.086 \times P_{CE})$$

The first two parentheticals are the direct effect and the indirect effect through challenger spending (the dashed arrows in figure 7.6), the sum of which is the nonexperience contribution to the expected effect, depicted as the solid dark gray line in figure 7.7. The final parenthetical is the effect of weighted challenger experience, depicted as the light gray line with circular markers. Note first that negative values of distributive spending (i.e., decreases in spending from one congress to the next) are associated with larger predicted probabilities of an experienced challenger's running, and therefore larger negative effects on vote share, but also positive effects on vote share through the nonexperience contribution—thus illustrating the countervailing forces referred to earlier. Overall, the slope of the total expected effect is negative, suggesting that increasing values of distributive spending lead to increasingly negative expected effects on vote share. There are two reasons for this. First, as distributive spending increases, the nonexperience contribution becomes increasingly negative. Second, even though the deterrence effect looks substantial, evidenced by the large decrease in the predicted probability of an experienced challenger's running, that probability is never zero. The weighted experience effect progressively shrinks, from its largest magnitude of −5.3 points to its smallest of −1.4 points, but at the highest values of distributive spending there is a substantial four-point decrease in vote share from the nonexperience-related effects of distributive spending.

I conclude this discussion of pork and Republican incumbents with an examination of the total effects of contingent liability awards on vote share, presented in figure 7.8. At both medium and high levels of polarization, contingent liabilities exert positive direct and indirect effects on incumbent vote share. In fact, the indirect effect, which works through a decrease in

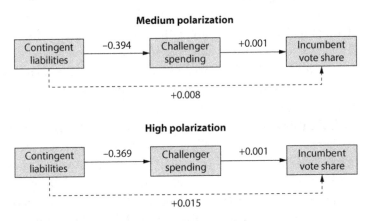

Medium polarization

Contingent liabilities → −0.394 → Challenger spending → +0.001 → Incumbent vote share

+0.008

High polarization

Contingent liabilities → −0.369 → Challenger spending → +0.001 → Incumbent vote share

+0.015

Total effect of a σ increase in contingent liability awards

At medium polarization: **+0.9 points**
At high polarization: **+1.6 points**

FIGURE 7.8 **Effects of contingent liability awards on Republican vote share**
Arrows identify the direct effects of contingent liability awards on incumbent vote share and the indirect effects through challenger spending. Similar to the previous flowcharts, the numbers signify the effects of an increase of one standard deviation in contingent liability awards. For example, under medium polarization, this increase in awards leads to a decrease of 0.394 in the natural log of challenger spending, which in turn leads to an increase of 0.001 (one-tenth of a point) in incumbent vote share. *Source*: Author's analysis of original data and data from American National Election Studies (2007, 2011, 2015), Bonica (2013a), Lewis et al. (2019), Roper Center for Public Opinion Research (2019), U.S. Bureau of the Census (n.d.), U.S. Bureau of Economic Analysis (2018), and U.S. Bureau of Fiscal Service (2019).

challenger spending, is roughly the same at both levels of polarization, an increase of one-tenth of a point in vote share. As discussed earlier, the direct effect of contingent liabilities increases with polarization; the effect nearly doubles moving from medium to high polarization. It is notable that contingent liabilities do not affect the vote share of Republican incumbents, either directly or indirectly, at lower levels of polarization. As expected, this conservative pork only begins to confer benefits when we move past lower levels of polarization. At a medium level of polarization, the total effect of a standard-deviation increase in the congress-difference in the natural log of contingent liability awards is nine-tenths of a point. When polarization is high, the total effect is 1.6 points, with the increase in magnitude coming entirely from the growth in the direct effect.

For Democrats, the only indirect effect that is relevant to the discussion of general-election vote share is the deterrent effect of distributive spending on the emergence of an experienced challenger when polarization is low. Holding all other variables at their mean or median values, an increase of one standard deviation in distributive spending decreases the predicted probability that an experienced challenger will run by 0.027, which, using the calculated total effect of challenger experience on vote share of −8.6 points, leads to an increase in expected vote share of roughly two-tenths of a point. Given that distributive spending has positive direct effects only when polarization is high, there is never a condition when securing distributive spending is harmful to Democratic incumbents. At low levels of polarization, pork barreling in this way can deter experienced challengers from running. At high levels of polarization, pork barreling directly increases vote shares. In between these two extremes, the results do not suggest an electoral benefit from pork barreling. It is highly unlikely in this context, however, that pork barreling Democrats are paying an electoral cost.

Conclusion

While each chapter so far has provided important information on the nuanced effects of the pork barrel in House elections, the focus of much scholarly attention is on election outcomes. The analysis of these outcomes, therefore, is where the steps of this work lead. The results presented in this chapter confirm a basic finding in the literature that members of different parties benefit from different types of pork. There are, however, several factors at work leading to the observed effects of the pork barrel on vote share. First, acknowledging that preferences for and responses to the pork barrel are based in ideology, there is a significant role for polarization in conditioning the effects of the pork barrel. The pork barrel generally has systematic partisan effects only when polarization is sufficiently high. This is a finding not previously considered by work on the pork barrel. For Democrats, explaining the electoral effects of the pork barrel is relatively straightforward. At higher levels of polarization, there is direct benefit from securing distributive spending. Pork barreling Democrats also spend less on their campaigns, which is recognized by the literature as a sign of incumbent safety. At lower levels of polarization, distributive spending deters experienced challengers from running, providing an indirect electoral benefit. Conversely, increases in contingent liability awards lead directly to lower vote shares for Democratic incumbents at any level of polarization.

For Republicans, as evidenced by the figures presented in this chapter, the story is more complex. At low levels of polarization, Republicans receive the same benefit as Democrats from distributive spending in the form of deterrence of experienced challengers. At higher levels of polarization, however, increases in distributive spending increase the likelihood of a contested primary, have no deterrent effects with respect to experienced general-election challengers, lead to increases in challenger spending independent of challenger experience, and bear direct electoral costs in terms of reduced vote share. All of these effects combine for a potentially positive relationship between distributive spending and vote share when polarization is low and a decidedly negative relationship at moderate and higher levels of polarization. With respect to contingent liabilities, or "Republican" pork, increasing awards at elevated levels of polarization directly increases Republican vote share, with the added bonus of lower spending by challengers.

Returning to the discussions from the first half of this work, these effects are firmly grounded in the ideological development of the parties and in the relationships between ideology, attitudes, and behavior among the mass public. Modern liberalism in the Democratic Party developed with an emphasis on using the power and resources of the federal government to better society. Projects and programs that use federal resources in an effort to create these better outcomes have become part of the liberal program. Modern conservatism in the Republican Party developed in opposition to these aspects of liberalism. Conservatism in the American tradition emphasizes the role of the individual, decrying the growth in size and influence of the federal government. While modern conservatism opposes the more commonly observable aspects of the pork barrel (i.e., direct payment and grant spending), it expresses a preference for government support of private behavior through contingent liabilities. In chapter 4, these ideological effects were observed in terms of preferences for government spending and in voting behavior, especially at higher levels of polarization. Conservatives, for example, are more likely to prefer less government spending when they live in districts that have seen increases in distributive spending. These individuals are also less likely to vote for their House incumbents. These results aid our understanding of the negative direct effects of distributive spending on the vote share of Republican incumbents. Why do Republicans who increase distributive spending in their districts receive a lower share of the vote? In part, it is because the conservatives who make up their electoral base are less likely to vote for them.

Conclusion

FOR DECADES, the conventional wisdom has held that legislators who bring funding back to their districts go a long way toward making themselves electorally safe. As I have detailed at various points, the empirical support for this belief has been mixed. In some work, mostly recent, pork barreling carries electoral benefits. In other work, securing spending on federal programs has no electoral effects at best or at worst can actually cost incumbent legislators votes. I argue that the inconsistent evidence is due to a misunderstanding of how the pork barrel affects the average voter. Rather than existing as a commodity-like benefit desired by all constituents, the pork barrel is, in the eyes of many voters, an aspect of the larger issue of government spending. As with the larger issue of spending, people develop preferences about the pork barrel based in part on ideology, leading to different effects of the pork barrel for incumbents of different parties.

Although prior work has recognized these partisan differences, it has failed to adequately account for the inconsistency we observe in the effects of the pork barrel over time. Despite long-standing ideological divisions over particularistic spending, I argue that the pork barrel is not regularly salient to the average voter. Polarization is the catalyst necessary for the pork barrel to affect electoral outcomes. It is only when the political world becomes more divided over everything else that the

153

average voter pays more attention to distributive spending, linking it to their more general preferences regarding government spending. During periods of low polarization, systematic general effects of the pork barrel are largely absent. When polarization is high, pork barrel spending affects primary competition, campaign spending, and ultimately vote share in general elections.

The discussions throughout this book advance the study of the electoral effects of distributive benefits in a number of ways. First, the conceptualization of the pork barrel as an issue differs from much of the literature and provides a stronger theoretical rationale for the partisan effects observed in prior studies than the more common explanation that different partisans in the public simply have different preferences regarding the type of pork they want legislators to pursue. Second, I provide a systematic explanation for variance in the effects of the pork barrel over time. These changes are not due only to differences in methodology between studies, but are also explained by varying levels of polarization across time. Third, the time period analyzed here is longer than it is in most other works. The election-year-level analysis examines almost a century-and-a-half of data on pork and election outcomes. The final three chapters include analyses of district-level data spanning fourteen elections. Finally, the individual-level analysis considers far more data than are typically presented in published works. The few works that examine the individual level tend to look only at a single election year, whereas this work includes data from 1986 through 2012. Fourth, this is one of the few works to look at district-level outcomes beyond incumbent vote share. The following sections provide detailed summaries of the findings, discuss the implications of these findings for elections and policy making, and present further questions and final thoughts.

The Pork Barrel and Ideology

Since the birth of the republic, federal spending has been an issue over which the parties have developed ideologically divergent positions. Support for or opposition to "internal improvements," as public works were called in the antebellum era, became central aspects of Democrat and Whig ideology and arguably one of the most divisive issues facing the parties besides slavery. The third chapter of this book concludes with an analysis of aggregate public-works spending and House election outcomes since the end of Reconstruction. The results show that Democratic incumbents perform better and Republican incumbents perform worse as national spending on public works increases, but only at sufficiently high levels of political polarization. Interestingly, the level of polarization at which public-works spending affects the electoral fortunes of Democrats is higher than for Republicans.

The theory expects that partisan differences in the electoral effects of the pork barrel are grounded in ideological differences made salient as polarization increases. The fourth chapter addresses this expectation at the individual level, considering the links between the pork barrel, polarization, attitudes, and behavior. I argue that as polarization increases, pork barrel spending is more consistently linked to broader attitudes on government spending in the mind of the voter, and the voter acts on this information in an ideologically consistent manner. The results demonstrate these connections. As distributive spending increases, respondents are more likely to identify government spending as the most important problem facing the country. Further, as polarization increases, the amount of distributive spending in the respondent's district becomes statistically linked to preferences for government spending and services and to vote choice. The findings most consistent with the theoretical expectations involve the attitudes and behavior of self-identified extreme conservatives, who both state preferences for less government spending and are less likely to vote for the incumbent as distributive spending increases. Coupling this observation with the result that public-works spending begins to affect the electoral fortunes of Republicans at lower levels of polarization as compared to Democrats opens the door to a Republican Party potentially affected in a wider variety of ways by the pork barrel. This is supported by work showing that polarization is asymmetric, with Republicans moving more to their extreme than Democrats, and it is borne out in the district-level analyses in this book.

Challengers, Campaigns, and Outcomes

Electoral motivations are central to our understanding of distributive politics. Polarization and the partisan-ideological sorting of voters that has accompanied it not only condition the electoral effects of the pork barrel, but polarization also shapes the pork barrel itself. Presumably election-minded legislators running for reelection in safe partisan districts dominated by ideologically extreme voters cater to this electorate in their pork barreling behavior. Polarization brings more contingent liabilities to Republican districts and more distributive spending to Democratic districts. Pursuing the "wrong" pork from an ideological perspective in a polarized environment has consequences. Consider, for instance, the role of distributive benefits in determining competition in primary elections. Primary losses by incumbents are extremely rare, but a loss is not the only way an incumbent can be damaged in a primary election. The literature on congressional primaries shows that competition itself tends to lead to worse performance in the general election. Whether there is resource drain or the risk of publicizing damaging information about the incumbent, the general conclusion is that incumbents who run for their party's nomination unopposed are in a better position than those who are challenged. Ideological positioning plays an important role in primary contestation, with incumbents who are less extreme than their districts more likely to face a challenge as polarization increases. Distributive spending, interestingly, works the same way, but only for Republicans. Just as being more liberal than constituents increases the risk of a challenge, so too does securing too much distributive spending.

The effects of the pork barrel on competition are not limited to primary elections. Considering the decisions of experienced politicians to challenge incumbents, these high-quality potential challengers are deterred from running by distributive spending when polarization is low. These politicians, many of whom have likely benefited from the pork barrel in their state and local elections, likely see this spending in its traditional, credit-claiming sense, bolstering the electoral safety of the legislators who secure it. When polarization is high, however, this deterrent effect, so prominent for Republicans in a low-polarization context, disappears. Just as potential primary challengers see distributive spending as a weakness of Republican incumbents when polarization is high, experienced politicians from the opposite party may follow the same logic. While distributive spending does not encourage experienced politicians to run when polarization is high, it at least no longer serves as a reason to avoid throwing one's hat in the ring.

Beyond challengers, the pork barrel affects campaign spending on the part of both candidates. Assuming the challengers' campaigns will be better funded and therefore engage in more spending when incumbents are weaker, and that incumbents themselves will spend more to shore up electoral weakness, the theoretical expectations regarding the pork barrel are largely supported. Distributive spending leads to less spending by Democratic incumbents and more spending by Republican incumbents and their challengers. Contingent liability awards decrease the campaign spending of Republican incumbents and their challengers. Incumbent spending does not significantly affect vote share in this examination, but several works cited in the sixth chapter show that increased campaign spending is associated with poorer performance for incumbents. Even in this work, increasing incumbent spending leads to a decreased likelihood of voting for the incumbent. All of these effects combine with direct effects on vote share, revealing relationships between the pork barrel and election outcomes that are conditioned by political polarization and consistent with an ideology-based view of the pork barrel. It is only as polarization increases that we observe general, systematic effects of the pork barrel on House elections, with incumbents benefiting from pork that is ideologically congruent with their party label.

Woe to the Spendthrift Republican

There is a more complex set of relationships between the pork barrel, polarization, and outcomes for Republicans than for Democrats. The explanation offered in various places and reiterated here is that government spending as an issue is a more central part of modern conservatism and thus more related to the fortunes of Republican incumbents. This is not to say that liberals are unconcerned with levels of government spending. The ideological focus of liberalism, however, has shifted significantly toward social outcomes over the past fifty years (Ellis and Stimson 2012). For Republicans, increasing distributive spending and polarization lead to increased primary competition, an increased likelihood of facing an experienced general-election challenger (relative to periods of low polarization), increased challenger spending, increased incumbent spending, and, ultimately, lower vote shares, due in part to decreased support from conservative voters. The deleterious effects of distributive spending, however, stand in contrast to the effects of contingent liability awards, or "conservative" pork, which benefit Republican incumbents through decreased challenger spending and by directly increasing vote share. For Democrats, the effects of the pork barrel are direct, ideologically consistent, and largely in conformity with my theoretical expectations. As polarization increases, distributive spending increases the vote share of incumbents. Contingent liabilities decrease the vote share of Democratic incumbents regardless of the level of polarization.

A reasonable question to ask at this point is why Republicans secure distributive spending above the normal amount for their districts when polarization is elevated. Relatedly, why do Democrats, who pursue any and all pork as polarization increases, ever bother securing contingent liability awards? As Fenno (1973) observes, legislators are motivated by a variety of goals. Some pork barreling surely has a policy focus for legislators. This book considers distributive spending and contingent liabilities aggregated by district. Individual programs, however, are meaningful to legislators and constituents. There is also a transactional aspect to the pork barrel, with influential groups, whether constituents, donors, or both, receiving legislator support for their pet projects and programs. Yet even policy-related goals have electoral implications, pork barreling included. On the distributive spending side, one possibility is that Republicans, and perhaps most members generally, pay the most attention to its deterrent effects. Even though this effect disappears at higher levels of polarization, many Republicans have served lengthy tenures in the House and have deterred strong politicians from challenging them in the past. The binary categorization of facing an experienced challenger or a political amateur is both highly visible and clearly related to election outcomes. It could also be that the pork barrel seems just a small part of the complex mechanics of electoral politics. As noted in the introductory chapter, in trying to determine the causes of a decrease in electoral performance, legislators do not likely place pork barreling high on the list. Even within the effects of the pork barrel, there are complex relationships undergirded by the ideological leanings of constituents and conditioned by political polarization. As the results make clear, however, Republican incumbents pay an electoral cost for securing distributive spending when polarization is at least at moderate levels. They benefit electorally from securing contingent liability awards. For Democrats, the opposite holds. They reap electoral benefits from distributive spending, especially at higher levels of polarization, and face costs for increases in contingent liability awards. This may be an artifact of the ideology of the incumbent. Chapter 2 reports that contingent liability awards increase with conservatism, particularly for Democrats. The district-level models control for legislator-district ideological congruence. The cost I find Democratic incumbents paying for contingent liability awards is potentially part of an additional cost of being conservative in a Democratic district.

Implications for the Legislative Process

That the pork barrel, which is really the geographic targeting of federal spending, carries different electoral implications in a polarized era is a meaningful conclusion for scholars of elections and of distributive politics. Despite this, one could argue that the practical implications of these findings are muted. Incumbents as a group seem to be just fine. While legislators may have fewer tools in the incumbency advantage box, they seem able to use their remaining tools to powerful effect. From 2000 to 2016, the average House reelection rate was 94 percent. At its lowest in the recent past, "only" 85 percent of House incumbents were reelected in 2010. The figure climbed back up to 90 percent in 2012, hitting 97 percent in 2016. Yet this change in the electoral usefulness of the pork barrel has real and important policy implications. "Trump Takes Infrastructure Pitch to Ohio As Sweeping Bill Stalls in Congress" read the headline of a news story in *The Hill* at the end of March 2018 (Shelbourne 2018). Despite the administration's plans to use limited federal funds to build partnerships with the private sector and to rely heavily on state and local funding, Congress has not shown much of an appetite for the president's proposal. Democrats have claimed that federal efforts do not go far enough, while majority Republicans have shied away from a massive infrastructure bill and the massive spending that goes along with it.

The preceding chapters point to a possible reason for the reluctance of Republicans to jump on board with the president's plan: large public-works projects, typical of the classic pork barrel, have no electoral value to the Republican Party in the polarized environment in which Congress operates. Most incumbents stay safe, but with drastically reduced federal investment in the nation's infrastructure. The preceding paragraph questioned continued Republican appetite for distributive spending. In the recent era, and particularly since regaining control of the House after the 2010 elections, many Republicans seem to have realized that supporting federal spending on infrastructure and similar projects has the potential to do more electoral harm than policy good.

The policy implications go well beyond public works. Whereas party leaders were previously able to use pork as a tangible benefit to trade for votes (Cann and Sidman 2011; Evans 2004), their reduced ability to do so has contributed to Congress's deteriorating productivity. In the decade of the 1980s, Congress enacted an average of 613 measures per congress. This dropped to 464 in the 1990s and 407 in the first decade of the twenty-first century. Since 2011, covering the 112th, 113th, and 114th congresses, this average has tumbled to 288, less than half of what it was just over twenty years ago (Stanley and Niemi 2015). The number of measures enacted is far from a perfect measure of congressional productivity, and a number of factors, such as the presence of divided government, help explain variation in congressional outputs. Anecdotally, however, the story has not been one of a hardworking Congress writing and passing a small number of time-consuming, society-changing pieces of legislation. Descriptions of Congress over the past several years tend to mirror the empirical reality: Congress has not accomplished much. The inability or unwillingness of party leaders to trade pork for support has contributed to this dearth of legislative activity.

Polarization, then, is doubly harmful to the legislative process. On its own, polarization correlates with increasing partisan animus (Mason

2015, 2018), leading members to resist working with any of their colleagues across the aisle, or with a president from the other party (Lee 2016). This is even the case when a party has in the past advocated for similar policies to those the other party now offers. As a basic example, consider Republican resistance to free trade agreements negotiated by the Obama administration. Beyond constant partisan warfare, polarization changes the electoral incentives of representatives. Members pay more attention to the ideologues in their districts and the extreme donors and activists that shape partisan opinions. From the perspective of the pork barrel, the electoral value of distributive spending decreases for Republicans as the value of contingent liabilities decreases for Democrats. Party leaders are limited in their ability to use the pork barrel to build bipartisan coalitions and would likely be punished for trying to do so anyway. The fact that pork has been used in this way in the past has led some in the media and Congress to speculate whether bringing back earmarks could improve the current situation in Congress (Davis 2018; Mundahl 2018). The results presented throughout this book suggest otherwise. Given the current majority, would members of the Freedom Caucus trade earmarks for votes, presumably on bills not meeting a threshold of conservatism? Probably not. Would Speaker Pelosi even offer earmarks to Republican members? Would Republicans make such a trade, handing Democratic leaders a policy victory? Again, this seems unlikely, suggesting that party leaders and policy entrepreneurs either need as yet unused tactics or an abatement to the current levels of political polarization.

Concluding Thoughts

While I have endeavored to present as thorough an examination of the electoral effects of the pork barrel on House elections as possible, there remain several fruitful avenues for examination. One relatively unexplored aspect of the electoral effects of distributive benefits is how constituents learn about and process information on the distributive activities of their representatives. Many works, including this one, assume that such a mechanism exists, given its centrality to the existence of electoral effects at all. The introductory chapter provided anecdotal accounts of how voters could be exposed to this information, but some scholars have cast doubt on how much voters could possibly know about benefits in their districts (e.g., Stein and Bickers 1994b). There has been some work examining credit claiming through election advertising and communications with the district (e.g., Basinger and Sidman 2007), and future research should continue in this vein.

An additional topic for future research is the link between interest groups, especially their campaign contributions and other election-related activities, and the pork barrel. My discussion in the sixth chapter cited a number of works on the contributions and expectations of donors, including the Rocca and Gordon (2013) examination of military pork. The empirical analyses I present, which consider the effects of aggregated pork barrel activity, approach the behavior of donors as rational actors giving more support to candidates with a greater likelihood of winning elections. In this context, where the pork barrel is harmful or helpful to the electoral fortunes of incumbents, challengers are better or worse funded, as reflected in their spending. Earlier in this conclusion, I alluded to the transactional nature of the pork barrel. Underlying the systematic effects of aggregated pork are individual groups with varying levels of influence trading their support, broadly construed, for tangible policy benefits, including federal spending on projects and programs. While such transactions in the aggregate might make it seem as though incumbents are working against their own electoral interests by pursuing these benefits, individually these transactions have a firm rational basis. The further study of these relationships would contribute much to our understanding of distributive politics.

Considering the "big picture," the discussion throughout this book points to a relatively straightforward empirical reality. Pork barreling, like many aspects of political life in the United States over the past decade and longer, is just another casualty of polarization. Normatively, some could argue this is good thing for society. Good riddance to wasteful spending on programs that benefit the few while the costs are borne by the many. While my district might suffer a little from lack of federal investment in certain projects and programs, society benefits because other districts suffer similarly and the federal government spends less. Interestingly, though, federal spending on distributive benefits, both distributive spending and contingent liability awards, has not decreased with Republican control first of the House, then of the Senate, and now of the presidency. As chapter 2 demonstrates, Democratic and Republican legislators actively pursue ideologically "correct" pork. Spending increases, but its distribution is more appropriately sorted. Another possible explanation for the continued increases in spending, not precluded by the first, is that while the Republican majority has eschewed spending on larger distributive projects, spending has increased across many smaller programs. Thus, spending goes up, but popular recognition of and reporting on this spending is low. Regardless of the reasons, the fact is that despite congressional efforts to reduce spending in many areas and the elimination of earmarks, the pork barrel persists. Polarization has changed legislative incentives regarding the pork barrel, and the true casualty seems to be policy itself. For the many who see this as a detriment to American political life, the solution is a broad rebuke of the partisan and personal invectives that have become so commonplace and a strong reaffirmation of our shared policy needs. How to achieve this, unfortunately, is a question our nation has largely avoided and seems unwilling to address.

Notes

1. Incumbents and Pork Barrel Politics

1. Senate Republicans would follow suit just after the midterm elections in November 2010.
2. Many of these studies employ data that start in 1983.
3. During the 110th Congress, committee reports were required to disclose earmark requests and their sponsors.
4. As the opening anecdote conveys, however, earmarking *is* currently banned.
5. This is similar to one explanation for the growth of distributive spending over time. With concentrated benefits and diffuse costs, the benefits to members for securing this spending tend to far outweigh the expected costs (Lowi 1964; Shepsle and Weingast 1981).

2. Pursuing the Pork Barrel

1. Cox and McCubbins (1993) would say these committees have targeted externalities; that is, their outputs generally affect committee members. Adler (2002) would further refer to this relationship in terms of high-demand, or constituent, committees. Certain committees represent policy areas that are of a higher demand for particular constituencies.
2. Their argument is based on their theory of conditional party government, which posits that parties and party leadership will be stronger when party members are

165

more homogenous in their preferences and the two parties are divergent in their preferences. The elite polarization is even more pronounced now than at the time of their first publications on the subject.

3. The spending decreases were in programs not directed at individuals. Entitlement programs targeting individual beneficiaries are what Bickers and Stein (2000) call "sacrosanct" and thus beyond substantial political manipulation.

4. All of the data analyzed in this book and all of the files necessary to replicate the results are available on my personal website, andrewsidman.com.

5. The National Science Foundation grant number is 0849883.

6. The scales use many variables in the *vcf08* series from the ANES-CDF. Scales for 2006 and 2010 use as many corresponding variables as could be identified. A full list of the items used in each year, details of how variables were recoded, and correlations between scales and the items from which they are derived are available at andrewsidman.com.

7. The most obvious way to control for general growth over time is by including time-period or congress dummy variables. This is not an option here, however, given the inclusion of polarization as a variable, which varies by election year. I opt instead for controlling for pork in the previous congress, including two congress dummies, and estimating models with robust standard errors.

8. Party unity scores were taken from Poole (2015).

9. The data on district characteristics from the 99th through 105th congresses were taken from Adler (n.d.). Data from the 106th through 112th congresses are based on my own coding of data from the U.S. Census Bureau.

10. In raw numbers, Republican districts received 117.7 more awards than Democratic districts. The natural log of awards is 0.39 higher in Republican districts. Both differences are significant beyond the 0.001 level.

11. The 90th percentile of DW-NOMINATE scores for Democrats, which should represent the ideology of the most conservative members of the party, has grown increasingly negative (more liberal) over the period analyzed here. The figure was −0.085 in the 99th Congress and climbed steadily to −0.233 in the 112th, which is the most liberal this figure has been since 1910.

12. These results are available from the author upon request.

3. An Electoral History of the Pork Barrel

1. Internal improvements, however, were less central to Hamilton's plan than were a central bank, assumption of state debts, and improving the overall credit of the new nation.

2. Military spending has been a constant and substantial component of government spending since the end of the Second World War, but, as argued in the previous

chapter, the mass public tends to hold attitudes regarding military spending that are distinct from attitudes on general government spending.

3. Hausman tests, reported in table 3.1, show no significant difference between models estimates using fixed effects and the random effects models reported here.

4. Public-works spending is a specific measure of what I have described as the type of spending that is preferred by modern liberals, but not by modern conservatives.

5. These publications are most commonly titled "Treasury Combined Statement of Receipts, Expenditures, and Balances of the United States Government." They are available as PDF files from the U.S. Government Publishing Office website: www.gpo.gov.

6. A 50–50 vote is one in which at least half of Democrats opposed at least half of Republicans.

7. Concerning the relationship between the two measures, there is also a question of whether mass polarization causes elite polarization, or vice versa, or whether the casual arrow points in both directions. Granger causality tests between the two series suggest that variation in the measure of mass polarization created here causes variation in the House polarization scale. Using the level form of both series and lags of one and two election years, mass polarization causes House polarization ($F = 3.88$, $p = 0.04$), but not vice versa ($F = 0.67$, $p = 0.52$). Using first differences produces the same substantive results: mass polarization causes House polarization ($F = 5.04$, $p = 0.02$), but not vice versa ($F = 0.17$, $p = 0.84$).

8. Data from 1929 through 2012 are from the U.S. Bureau of Economic Analysis (2018). Data prior to 1929 are taken from Johnston and Williamson (2019).

9. The following wars are included: the Spanish-American War (1898), World War I (1918), World War II (1942, 1944), the Korean War (1950, 1952), the Vietnam War (1964–1974), and the wars in Afghanistan and Iraq (2002–2012).

10. There are no scholarly definitions of a "wave" election. The term has been used in some recent publications, often in recognition of a year like 2010 as a wave year. In a post on *Sabato's Crystal Ball*, Abramowitz (2011) defines wave elections as those "in which one party makes substantial gains in the House and Senate." I decided on a gain of 10 percent of the seats in the House in an effort to quantify "substantial" in a way that is not overly inclusive. Democratic wave years are 1874, 1890, 1910, 1912, 1922, 1930, 1932, 1948, 1958, and 1974. Republican wave years are 1894, 1904, 1920, 1938, 1942, 1946, 1966, 1994, and 2010.

4. Attitudes, Voting, and the Pork Barrel

1. Feldman and Steenbergen (2001) note the differences between egalitarianism and humanitarianism as value orientations. Egalitarianism pushes individuals toward preferring sweeping economic intervention, while those for whom

humanitarian values are more important prefer less intrusive programs targeting the needy.

2. For the period examined in the individual- and district-level analyses (1986 through 2012), the question is worded as follows: "What do you think are the most important problems facing this country?" Responses are coded into the variable *vcf0875b*.
3. It is certainly the case that these variables have either opposite effects, as candidates emphasize other issues as important problems, or no effects at all.
4. Individuals unable to place themselves on the ideological identification scale are excluded from the analyses in this chapter.
5. The question is most often worded as follows: "Some people think the government should provide fewer services, even in areas such as health and education, in order to reduce spending. Other people feel that it is important for the government to provide many more services even if it means an increase in spending. Where would you place yourself on this scale, or haven't you thought much about this?"
6. The question asks: "If you had a say in making up the federal budget this year, for which of the following programs would you like to see spending increased and for which would you like to see spending decreased: should federal spending on welfare programs be increased, decreased, or kept about the same?" Responses of decreased were coded as −1, kept about the same as 0, and increased as 1.

5. Challenges from Within the Party

1. Data on primary losses are taken from casualty lists published by *Roll Call*.
2. Data on primary elections were collected from the Federal Election Commission.
3. Brady, Han, and Pope (2007) find that the incumbent's lagged general-election vote share leads to an increase in primary competition, while lagged primary-vote share leads to less competition. Lagged general-election vote share in their analysis is likely picking up on party advantage in the district, while lagged primary-vote share measures the incumbent's electoral strength. My model appears to be tapping the same effects, with the partisan normal vote measuring party strength and lagged vote share measuring incumbent strength.
4. Closed-primary states, as identified by the National Conference of State Legislatures (2018), are Delaware, Florida, Kansas, Kentucky, Maine, Nevada, New Jersey, New Mexico, New York, Pennsylvania, and Wyoming.
5. States are coded 1 if in a given election year there is at least one legislator ineligible to run for either chamber (or in the case of Nebraska, the only chamber) of the state legislature because of statutory term limits. The states that have had legislators affected by term limits at any point in the time period examined here are Arizona, Arkansas, California, Colorado, Florida, Louisiana, Maine, Michigan,

Missouri, Montana, Nebraska, Nevada, Ohio, Oklahoma, Oregon, and South Dakota. The list of states—including the years in which term limits were enacted, years of impact, and, in six cases, repealed—can be obtained from the National Conference of State Legislatures (2015).

6. Calculations of the marginal effects and predicted probabilities discussed in this section hold all other variables at their mean or median values for continuous and categorical variables, respectively.

7. The distributive spending variable has a full range of −4.4 to 5.3. The extreme values, however, are outliers. The effective range encompasses all observations between the 5th and 95th percentiles.

6. General-Election Challengers and Campaigns

1. This is not to suggest that these types of pork are mutually exclusive. Districts certainly receive a mix of both types, although representatives may gain a reputation for securing a particular type of project.

2. See also Gerber (1998) and Green and Krasno (1990).

3. The more natural first step in the analysis, given this logic, would be an analysis of challenger receipts. Much of the work on the electoral effects of campaign funds, however, focuses on spending. This is my focus as well, particularly given the analysis of vote share in the next chapter. For the challenger, the correlation between campaign receipts and campaign spending is 0.9996 in these data, suggesting that the two figures are nearly identical. I also estimate the challenger spending model described later in this chapter using the natural log of challenger receipts as the dependent variable. In a seemingly unrelated estimation between the two models, which allows for the clustering of standard errors by election year and comparison of coefficients between equations, there was no pair of coefficients between models whose difference was significant at or beyond the 0.05 level.

4. There is empirical work supporting the "vote buying" hypothesis in particular policy domains, exemplified by Stratmann (1991, 1998, 2002) and Fleisher (1993).

5. The excluded indicators of challenger experience include those independent variables from that model that are not included in the challenger or incumbent spending models: whether the incumbent was a freshman in the congress preceding the election, whether the incumbent represents a district in a southern state, whether the state has closed primaries, whether the state has legislators impacted by term limits, and whether it is a redistricting year.

6. There is also the practical reality that amateur challengers do not spend much on their campaigns. The results of the challenger spending model show that experienced challengers spend 140.6 percent more than amateurs, all else being equal. With respect to actual spending, between 1986 and 2012, mean real spending

by experienced challengers was $695,405.20 and the mean for amateurs was $267,660.60. To highlight the discrepancy further, 80 percent of amateur challengers spent less than $346,000 on their campaigns. This amount is surpassed by the 46th percentile among experienced challengers.

7. Election Outcomes

1. The dichotomous variables are estimated via probit using all of the variables from the vote share equation and the following excluded variables: the number of terms the incumbent served in the House (contested primary), the interaction of presidential party with the annual percentage change in second quarter RGDP (contested primary), whether the incumbent is a freshman (challenger experience), an indicator for southern states (challenger experience), its interaction with incumbent party (contested primary), closed primary state (both), term limits for state legislators (both), and an indicator for redistricting years (contested primary). The instrument used the in 2SLS analysis is the predicted probability from the probit estimation that the dichotomous variable equals 1.

2. With respect to endogeneity, the F-statistic equals 11.713, which is significant beyond the 0.1 percent level and suggests that the variables are endogenous. The Sargan χ^2 test of overidentifying restrictions, for which a significant result suggests that instruments are invalid, equals 0.461 and has a p-value equal to 0.497. The endogeneity test was conducted on the system of equations presented here, which include standard errors adjusted for clustering by election year. Instrument tests in Stata 11 cannot be conducted with adjusted standard errors; the Sargan test, therefore, was estimated on the same system of equations estimated via 2SLS with conventional standard errors.

3. The basic idea is that the deterrence effect should be strongest for the weakest incumbents. Strong incumbents will have (and do have) a small likelihood of facing an experienced challenger regardless of the value of distributive spending. To be sure, increases in spending further decrease this likelihood, but the deterrence effect will be smaller in magnitude than for weaker incumbents, given that predicted effects in probit models are conditional on values of the other independent variables.

References

Abramowitz, Alan I. 1988. "Explaining Senate Election Outcomes." *American Political Science Review* 82, no. 2: 385–403.

——. 1991. "Incumbency, Campaign Spending, and the Decline of Competition in U.S. House Elections." *Journal of Politics* 53, no. 1: 34–56.

——. 2011. "The Anti-Incumbent Election Myth: Or Why You Shouldn't Hold Your Breath Waiting for a 'Triple Flip' Election." *Sabato's Crystal Ball*, December 22. http://www.centerforpolitics.org/crystalball/articles/the-anti-incumbent-election-myth/.

——. 2015. "The New American Electorate: Partisan, Sorted, and Polarized." In *American Gridlock: The Sources, Character, and Impact of Political Polarization*, ed. James A. Thurber and Antoine Yoshinaka, 19–44. New York: Cambridge University Press.

Abramowitz, Alan I., and Kyle L. Saunders. 2008. "Is Polarization a Myth?" *Journal of Politics* 70, no. 2: 542–555.

Abramson, Paul R. 1976. "Generational Change and the Decline of Party Identification in America: 1952–1974." *American Political Science Review* 70, no. 2: 469–478.

Adams, James, and Samuel Merrill III. 2008. "Candidate and Party Strategies in Two-Stage Elections Beginning with a Primary." *American Journal of Political Science* 52, no. 2: 344–359.

——. n.d. Congressional District Data File, 98th to 105th Congresses. Boulder: University of Colorado.

Adler, E. Scott. 2002. *Why Congressional Reforms Fail: Reelection and the House Committee System*. Chicago: University of Chicago Press.

Aldrich, John H. 1995. *Why Parties? The Origin and Transformation of Political Parties in America*. Chicago: University of Chicago Press.

Aldrich, John H., and David W. Rohde. 1997. "The Transition to Republican Rule in the House: Implications for Theories of Congressional Politics." *Political Science Quarterly* 112, no. 4: 541–567.

——. 2005. "Congressional Committees in a Partisan Era." In *Congress Reconsidered*, ed. Lawrence C. Dodd and Bruce I. Oppenheimer, 249–270. Washington, DC: CQ Press.

Alvarez, R. Michael, and Jason L. Saving. 1997a. "Congressional Committees and the Political Economy of Federal Outlays." *Public Choice* 92: 55–73.

——. 1997b. "Deficits, Democrats, and Distributive Benefits: Congressional Elections and the Pork Barrel in the 1980s." *Political Research Quarterly* 50, no. 4: 809–831.

American National Election Studies. 2007. 2006 Pilot Study. Stanford, CA: Stanford University; Ann Arbor: University of Michigan. www.electionstudies.org.

——. 2011. 2010 Panel Recontact Study. Stanford, CA: Stanford University; Ann Arbor: University of Michigan. www.electionstudies.org.

——. 2015. Time Series Cumulative Data File 1948–2012. Stanford, CA: Stanford University; Ann Arbor: University of Michigan. www.electionstudies.org.

Anagnoson, J. Theodore. 1982. "Federal Grant Agencies and Congressional Election Campaigns." *American Journal of Political Science* 26, no. 3: 547–561.

Ansolabehere, Stephen, John M. de Figueiredo, and James M. Snyder Jr. 2003. "Why Is There So Little Money in U.S. Politics?" *Journal of Economic Perspectives* 17, no. 1: 105–130.

Arceneaux, Kevin, and Martin Johnson. 2015. "More a Symptom Than a Cause: Polarization and Partisan News Media in America." In *American Gridlock: The Sources, Character, and Impact of Political Polarization*, ed. James A. Thurber and Antoine Yoshinaka, 309–336. New York: Cambridge University Press.

Arnold, R. Douglas. 1990. *The Logic of Congressional Action*. New Haven, CT: Yale University Press.

Austen-Smith, David. 1995. "Campaign Contributions and Access." *American Political Science Review* 89, no. 3: 566–581.

Balla, Steven J., Eric D. Lawrence, Forrest Maltzman, and Lee Sigelman. 2002. "Partisanship, Blame Avoidance, and the Distribution of Legislative Pork." *American Journal of Political Science* 46, no. 3: 515–525.

Basinger, Scott J., and Michael J. Ensley. 2007. "Candidates, Campaigns, or Partisan Conditions? Reevaluating Strategic-Politicians Theory." *Legislative Studies Quarterly* 32, no. 3: 361–394.

Basinger, Scott J., and Andrew. H. Sidman. 2007. "Campaign Advertising and Credit Claiming in the 2002 Congressional Elections." Presented at the annual meeting of the Midwest Political Science Association, Chicago.

Berry, Christopher R., Barry C. Burden, and William G. Howell. 2010a. "After Enactment: The Lives and Deaths of Federal Programs." *American Journal of Political Science* 54, no. 1: 1–17.

——. 2010b. "The President and the Distribution of Federal Spending." *American Political Science Review* 104, no. 4: 783–799.

Bertelli, Anthony M., and Christian R. Grose. 2009. "Secretaries of Pork? A New Theory of Distributive Public Policy." *Journal of Politics* 71, no. 3: 926–945.

Bickers, Kenneth N. 1991. "The Programmatic Expansion of the U.S. Government." *Western Political Quarterly* 44, no. 4: 891–914.

Bickers, Kenneth N., Diana Evans, Robert M. Stein, and Robert D. Wrinkle. 2007. "The New and Old Electoral Connection: Earmarks and Pork Barrel Politics." Presented at the annual meeting of the Midwest Political Science Association, Chicago.

Bickers, Kenneth N., and Robert M. Stein. 1996. "The Electoral Dynamics of the Federal Pork Barrel." *American Journal of Political Science* 40, no. 4: 1300–1326.

——. 2000. "The Congressional Pork Barrel in a Republican Era." *Journal of Politics* 62, no. 4: 1070–1086.

Binder, Sarah A. 1999. "The Dynamics of Legislative Gridlock, 1947–96." *American Political Science Review* 93, no. 3: 519–533.

Black, Duncan. 1958. *A Theory of Committees and Elections.* New York: Cambridge University Press.

Bond, Jon R., Cary Covington, and Richard Fleisher. 1985. "Explaining Challenger Quality in Congressional Elections." *Journal of Politics* 47, no. 2: 510–529.

Bonica, Adam. 2013a. Database on Ideology, Money in Politics, and Elections: Public version 1.0 [computer file]. Stanford, CA: Stanford University Libraries. http://data.stanford.edu/dime.

——. 2013b. "Ideology and Interests in the Political Marketplace." *American Journal of Political Science* 57, no. 2: 294–311.

——. 2014. "Mapping the Ideological Marketplace." *American Journal of Political Science* 58, no. 2: 367–387.

Bonica, Adam, Nolan McCarty, Keith T. Poole, and Howard Rosenthal. 2015. "Congressional Polarization and Its Connection to Income Inequality: An Update." In *American Gridlock: The Sources, Character, and Impact of Political Polarization*, ed. James A. Thurber and Antoine Yoshinaka, 357–377. New York: Cambridge University Press.

Born, Richard. 1981. "The Influence of House Primary Election Divisiveness on General Election Margins, 1962–76." *Journal of Politics* 43, no. 3: 640–661.

Bowman, Bridget. 2016. "A Tale of Two Bars." *Roll Call*, April 25. http://www.rollcall.com/news/politics/tale-two-bars.

Brady, David W., Joseph Cooper, and Patricia A. Hurley. 1979. "The Decline of Party in the U.S. House of Representatives, 1887–1968." *Legislative Studies Quarterly* 4, no. 3: 381–407.

Brady, David W., Hahrie Han, and Jeremy C. Pope. 2007. "Primary Elections and Candidate Ideology: Out of Step with the Primary Electorate?" *Legislative Studies Quarterly* 32, no. 1: 79–105.

Bronars, Stephen G., and John R. Lott Jr. 1997. "Do Campaign Donations Alter How a Politician Votes? Or, Do Donors Support Candidates Who Value the Same Things That They Do?" *Journal of Law and Economics* 40, no. 2: 317–350.

Burden, Barry. 2001. "The Polarizing Effects of Congressional Primaries." In *Congressional Primaries and the Politics of Representation*, ed. Peter F. Galderisi, Marni Ezra, and Michael Lyons, 48–61. Lanham, MD: Rowman & Littlefield.

——. 2004. "Candidate Positioning in US Congressional Elections." *British Journal of Political Science* 34, no. 2: 211–227.

Cain, Bruce, John Ferejohn, and Morris Fiorina. 1987. *The Personal Vote: Constituency Service and Electoral Independence*. Cambridge, MA: Harvard University Press.

Campbell, Angus, Philip E. Converse, Warren E. Miller, and Donald E. Stokes. 1960. *The American Voter*. Chicago: University of Chicago Press.

Canes-Wrone, Brandice, David W. Brady, and John F. Cogan. 2002. "Out of Step, Out of Office: Electoral Accountability and House Members' Voting." *American Political Science Review* 96, no. 1: 127–140.

Cann, Damon M. 2008. *Sharing the Wealth: Member Contributions and the Exchange Theory of Party Influence in the U.S. House of Representatives*. Albany: State University of New York Press.

Cann, Damon M., and Andrew H. Sidman. 2011. "Exchange Theory, Political Parties, and the Allocation of Federal Distributive Benefits in the House of Representatives." *Journal of Politics* 73, no. 4: 1128–1141.

Carey, John M., Richard G. Niemi, and Lynda W. Powell. 1998. "The Effects of Term Limits on State Legislatures." *Legislative Studies Quarterly* 23, no. 2: 271–300.

Carmines, Edward G., Michael J. Ensley, and Michael W. Wagner. 2012. "Who Fits the Left-Right Divide? Partisan Polarization in the American Electorate." *American Behavioral Scientist* 56, no. 12: 1631–1653.

Carsey, Thomas M., and Barry Rundquist. 1999. "Party and Committee in Distributive Politics: Evidence from Defense Spending." *Journal of Politics* 61, no. 4: 1156–1169.

Carson, Jamie L. 2005. "Strategy, Selection, and Candidate Competition in U.S. House and Senate Elections." *Journal of Politics* 67, no. 1: 1–28.

Carson, Jamie, Michael H. Crespin, Carrie P. Eaves, and Emily O. Wanless. 2012. "Constituency Congruency and Candidate Competition in Primary Elections for the U.S. House." *State Politics & Policy Quarterly* 12, no. 2: 127–145.

Cashman, Sean D. 1993. *America in the Gilded Age: From the Death of Lincoln to the Rise of Theodore Roosevelt*. 3rd ed. New York: New York University Press.

Chappell, Henry W., Jr. 1982. "Campaign Contributions and Congressional Voting: A Simultaneous Probit-Tobit Model." *Review of Economics and Statistics* 64, no. 1: 77–83.

Chen, Jowei. 2010. "The Effect of Electoral Geography on Pork Barreling in Bicameral Legislatures." *American Journal of Political Science* 54, no. 2: 301–322.

——. 2013. "Voter Partisanship and the Effect of Distributive Spending on Political Participation." *American Journal of Political Science* 57, no. 1: 200–217.

Clarke, David, and Edward Epstein. 2010. "Earmark Bans Get a Frosty Reception." *CQ Weekly*, March 15, 634.

Conover, Pamela J., and Stanley Feldman. 1981. "The Origins and Meaning of Liberal /Conservative Self-Identification." *American Journal of Political Science* 25, no. 4: 617–645.

Converse, Philip E. 1964. "The Nature of Belief Systems in Mass Publics." In *Ideology and Discontent*, ed. David Apter, 206–261. New York: Free Press.

Cox, Gary W., and Mathew D. McCubbins. 1993. *Legislative Leviathan: Party Government in the House*. Berkeley: University of California Press.

Crespin, Michael H., and Charles J. Finocchiaro. 2013. "Elections and the Politics of Pork in the U.S. Senate." *Social Science Quarterly* 94, no. 2: 506–529.

Currinder, Marian L. 2003. "Leadership PAC Contribution Strategies and House Member Ambitions." *Legislative Studies Quarterly* 28, no. 4: 551–577.

Davis, Susan. 2018. "Lawmakers Testify at Hearing: Bring Earmarks Back." *National Public Radio*, January 18. https://www.npr.org/2018/01/18/578655381/lawmakers -testify-at-hearing-bring-earmarks-back.

Dionne, E. J., Jr. 1992. *Why Americans Hate Politics*. New York: Simon and Schuster.

Dominguez, Casey B. K. 2011. "Does the Party Matter? Endorsements in Congressional Primaries." *Political Research Quarterly* 64, no. 3: 534–544.

Downs, Anthony. 1957. *An Economic Theory of Democracy*. Boston: Addison Wesley.

Druckman, James N. 2004. "Priming the Vote: Campaign Effects in a U.S. Senate Election." *Political Psychology* 25, no. 4: 577–594.

Ellickson, Mark C., and Donald E. Whistler. 2001. "Explaining State Legislators' Casework and Public Resource Allocation." *Political Research Quarterly* 54, no. 3: 553–569.

Ellis, Christopher, and James A. Stimson. 2012. *Ideology in America*. New York: Cambridge University Press.

Engstrom, Erik J., and Georg Vanberg. 2010. "Assessing the Allocation of Pork: Evidence from Congressional Earmarks." *American Politics Research* 38, no. 6: 959–985.

Erikson, Robert S., and Gerald C. Wright Jr. 1980. "Policy Representation of Constituency Interests." *Political Behavior* 2, no. 1: 91–106.

Evans, Diana. 1994. "Policy and Pork: The Use of Pork Barrel Projects to Build Policy Coalitions in the House of Representatives." *American Journal of Political Science* 38, no. 4: 894–917.

——. 2004. *Greasing the Wheels: Using Pork Barrel Projects to Build Majority Coalitions in Congress*. Cambridge: Cambridge University Press.

Executive Office of the President of the United States. Office of Management and Budget. 2012. *Catalog of Federal Domestic Assistance*. Washington, DC: General Services Administration.

——. 2015. *Fiscal Year 2016 Historical Tables: Budget of the U.S. Government.* Washington, DC: Government Printing Office.

Ezra, Marni. 2001. "The Benefits and Burdens of Congressional Primary Elections." In *Congressional Primaries and the Politics of Representation*, ed. Peter F. Galderisi, Marni Ezra, and Michael Lyons, 48–61. Lanham, MD: Rowman & Littlefield.

Feldman, Paul, and James Jondrow. 1984. "Congressional Elections and Local Federal Spending." *American Journal of Political Science* 28, no. 1: 147–164.

Feldman, Stanley. 1988. "Structure and Consistency in Public Opinion: The Role of Core Beliefs and Values." *American Journal of Political Science* 32, no. 2: 416–440.

Feldman, Stanley, and Marco R. Steenbergen. 2001. "The Humanitarian Foundation of Public Support for Social Welfare." *American Journal of Political Science* 45, no. 3: 658–677.

Feldman, Stanley, and John Zaller. 1992. "The Political Culture of Ambivalence: Ideological Responses to the Welfare State." *American Journal of Political Science* 36, no. 1: 268–307.

Fenno, Richard F., Jr. 1973. *Congressmen in Committees*. Boston: Little, Brown.

——. 1978. *Home Style: House Members in Their Districts.* Boston: Little, Brown.

Ferejohn, John A. 1974. *Pork Barrel Politics: Rivers and Harbors Legislation, 1947–1968.* Stanford, CA: Stanford University Press.

Fiorina, Morris P. 1981. "Some Problems in Studying the Effects of Resource Allocation in Congressional Elections." *American Journal of Political Science* 25, no. 3: 543–567.

Fiorina, Morris P., Samuel J. Abrams, and Jeremy C. Pope. 2006. *Culture War? The Myth of a Polarized America.* 2nd ed. New York: Pearson Longman.

Fleisher, Richard. 1993. "PAC Contributions and Congressional Voting on National Defense." *Legislative Studies Quarterly* 18, no. 3: 391–409.

Fouirnaies, Alexander, and Andrew B. Hall. 2014. "The Financial Incumbency Advantage." *Journal of Politics* 76, no. 3: 711–724.

Fox, Justin, and Lawrence Rothenberg. 2011. "Influence Without Bribes: A Noncontracting Model of Campaign Giving and Policymaking." *Political Analysis* 19, no. 3: 325–341.

Garner, Andrew, and Harvey Palmer. 2011. "Polarization and Issue Consistency Over Time." *Political Behavior* 33, no. 2: 225–246.

Gerber, Alan. 1998. "Estimating the Effects of Campaign Spending on Senate Election Outcomes Using Instrumental Variables." *American Political Science Review* 92, no. 2: 401–411.

Gerber, Alan S., James G. Gimpel, Donald P. Green, and Daron R. Shaw. 2011. "How Large and Long-Lasting Are the Persuasive Effects of Televised Campaign Ads? Results from a Randomized Field Experiment." *American Political Science Review* 105, no. 1: 135–150.

Goldstein, Ken, and Paul Freedman. 2000. "New Evidence for New Arguments: Money and Advertising in the 1996 Senate Elections." *Journal of Politics* 62, no. 4: 1087–1108.

Goodliffe, Jay, and David B. Magleby. 2001. "Campaign Finance in U.S. House Primary and General Elections." In *Congressional Primaries and the Politics of Representation*, ed. Peter F. Galderisi, Marni Ezra, and Michael Lyons, 62–76. Lanham, MD: Rowman & Littlefield.

Gordon, Sanford C., and Hannah K. Simpson. 2018. "The Birth of Pork: Local Appropriations in America's First Century." *American Political Science Review* 112, no. 3: 564–579.

Goss, Carol F. 1972. "Military Committee Membership and Defense-Related Benefits in the House of Representatives." *Western Political Quarterly* 25, no. 2: 215–233.

Green, Donald P., and Jonathan S. Krasno. 1988. "Salvation for the Spendthrift Incumbent: Reestimating the Effects of Campaign Spending in House Elections." *American Journal of Political Science* 32, no. 4: 884–907.

——. 1990. "Rebuttal to Jacobson's 'New Evidence for Old Arguments.' " *American Journal of Political Science* 34, no. 2: 363–372.

Green, John C. 2001. "Elections and Amateurs: The Christian Right in the 1998 Congressional Campaigns." In *Congressional Primaries and the Politics of Representation*, ed. Peter F. Galderisi, Marni Ezra, and Michael Lyons, 77–91. Lanham, MD: Rowman & Littlefield.

Grier, Kevin B. 1989. "Campaign Spending and Senate Elections, 1978–84." *Public Choice* 63, no. 3: 201–219.

Grimmer, Justin. 2013. "Appropriators Not Position Takers: The Distorting Effects of Electoral Incentives on Congressional Representation." *American Journal of Political Science* 57, no. 3: 624–642.

Grimmer, Justin, Solomon Messing, and Sean J. Westwood. 2012. "How Words and Money Cultivate a Personal Vote: The Effect of Legislator Credit Claiming on Constituent Credit Allocation." *American Political Science Review* 106, no. 4: 703–719.

Hamman, John A. 1993. "Universalism, Program Development, and the Distribution of Federal Assistance." *Legislative Studies Quarterly* 18, no. 4: 553–568.

Hamman, John A., and Jeffrey E. Cohen. 1997. "Reelection and Congressional Support: Presidential Motives in Distributive Politics." *American Politics Research* 25, no. 1: 56–74.

Harden, Jeffrey J., and Justin H. Kirkland. 2016. "Do Campaign Donors Influence Polarization? Evidence from Public Financing in the American States." *Legislative Studies Quarterly* 41, no. 1: 119–152.

Hartz, Louis. 1955. *The Liberal Tradition in America: An Interpretation of American Political Thought Since the Revolution*. New York: Harcourt Brace.

Hayes, Danny, and Jennifer L. Lawless. 2015. "News as a Casualty: District Polarization and Media Coverage of U.S. House Campaigns." In *American Gridlock: The Sources, Character, and Impact of Political Polarization*, ed. James A. Thurber and Antoine Yoshinaka, 287–308. New York: Cambridge University Press.

Heidler, David S., and Jeanne T. Heidler. 2010. *Henry Clay: The Essential American.* New York: Random House.

Herrnson, Paul S., and James G. Gimpel. 1995. "District Conditions and Primary Divisiveness in Congressional Elections." *Political Research Quarterly* 48, no. 1: 117–134.

Hetherington, Marc J. 1996. "The Media's Role in Forming Voters' National Economic Evaluations in 1992." *American Journal of Political Science* 40, no. 2: 372–395.

——. 2001. "Resurgent Mass Partisanship: The Role of Elite Polarization." *American Political Science Review* 95, no. 3: 619–631.

Hirano, Shigeo, James M. Snyder Jr., and Michael M. Ting. 2009. "Distributive Politics with Primaries." *Journal of Politics* 71, no. 4: 1467–1480.

Hird, John. 1991. "The Political Economy of Pork: Project Selection at U.S. Corps of Army Engineers." *American Political Science Review* 85, no. 2: 429–456.

Holt, Michael F. 1999. *The Rise and Fall of the American Whig Party: Jacksonian Politics and the Onset of the Civil War.* New York: Oxford University Press.

Hoover, Kenneth R., John Miles, Vernon Johnson, and Sara Weir. 2001. *Ideology and Political Life.* 3rd ed. Belmont, CA: Wadsworth.

Hostetler, Michael J. 2011. "The Early American Quest for Internal Improvements: Distance and Debate." *Rhetorica: A Journal of the History of Rhetoric* 29, no. 1: 53–75.

Howe, Daniel W. 2007. *What Hath God Wrought: The Transformation of America, 1815–1848.* New York: Oxford University Press.

Iyengar, Shanto, and Sean J. Westwood. 2015. "Fear and Loathing Across Party Lines: New Evidence on Group Polarization." *American Journal of Political Science* 59, no. 3: 690–707.

Jackson, Andrew. 1830. "Veto Message, May 27, 1830." *The American Presidency Project.* Accessed May 9, 2018. https://www.presidency.ucsb.edu/documents/veto -message-471.

Jacobson, Gary C. 1978. "The Effects of Campaign Spending in Congressional Elections." *American Political Science Review* 72, no. 2: 469–491.

——. 1989. "Strategic Politicians and the Dynamics of U.S. House Elections, 1946–86." *American Political Science Review* 83, no. 3: 773–793.

——. 1990. "The Effects of Campaign Spending in House Elections: New Evidence for Old Arguments." *American Journal of Political Science* 34, no. 2: 334–362.

——. 1996. "The 1994 House Elections in Perspective." *Political Science Quarterly* 111, no. 2: 203–223.

——. 2015. "Partisan Media and Electoral Polarization in 2012: Evidence from the American National Election Study." In *American Gridlock: The Sources, Character, and Impact of Political Polarization*, ed. James A. Thurber and Antoine Yoshinaka, 259–286. New York: Cambridge University Press.

Jacoby, William G. 2000. "Issue Framing and Public Opinion on Government Spending." *American Journal of Political Science* 44, no. 4: 750–767.

Jewell, Malcolm E., and David Breaux. 1991. "Southern Primary and Electoral Competition and Incumbent Success." *Legislative Studies Quarterly* 16, no. 1: 129–143.

Johannes, John R. 1980. "The Distribution of Casework in the U.S. Congress: An Uneven Burden." *Legislative Studies Quarterly* 5, no. 4: 517–544.

——. 1983a. "Explaining Congressional Casework Styles." *American Journal of Political Science* 27, no. 3: 530–547.

——. 1983b. "Political Culture & Congressional Constituency Styles." *Polity* 15, no. 4: 555–572.

Johannes, John R., and John C. McAdams. 1981. "The Congressional Incumbency Effect: Is It Casework, Policy Compatibility, or Something Else? An Examination of the 1978 Election." *American Journal of Political Science* 25, no. 3: 512–542.

Johnston, Louis, and Samuel H. Williamson. 2019. "What Was the U.S. GDP Then?." MeasuringWorth.com. https://www.measuringworth.com/usgdp/.

Kalla, Joshua L., and David E. Broockman. 2016. "Campaign Contributions Facilitate Access to Congressional Officials: A Randomized Field Experiment." *American Journal of Political Science* 60, no. 3: 545–558.

Kenney, Patrick J. 1988. "Sorting Out the Effects of Primary Divisiveness in Congressional and Senatorial Elections." *Western Political Quarterly* 41, no. 4: 765–777.

Key, V. O., Jr. 1955. "A Theory of Critical Elections." *Journal of Politics* 17, no. 1: 3–18.

Kiewiet, D. Roderick, and Mathew D. McCubbins. 1988. "Presidential Influence on Congressional Appropriations Decisions." *American Journal of Political Science* 32, no. 3: 713–736.

King, Gary. 1995. Elections to the United States House of Representatives, 1898–1992 [computer file]. ICPSR version. Ann Arbor, MI: Inter-university Consortium for Political and Social Research.

Krasno, Jonathan S., and Donald P. Green. 1988. "Preempting Quality Challengers in House Elections." *Journal of Politics* 50, no. 4: 920–936.

Krasno, Jonathan S., Donald P. Green, and Jonathan A. Cowden. 1994. "The Dynamics of Campaign Fundraising in House Elections." *Journal of Politics* 56, no. 2: 459–474.

Krehbiel, Keith. 1993. "Where's the Party?" *British Journal of Political Science* 23, no. 2: 235–266.

Kriner, Douglas L., and Andrew Reeves. 2012. "The Influence of Federal Spending on Presidential Elections." *American Political Science Review* 106, no. 2: 348–366.

——. 2015. *The Particularistic President: Executive Branch Politics and Political Inequality.* New York: Cambridge University Press.

Langbein, Laura I. 1986. "Money and Access: Some Empirical Evidence." *Journal of Politics* 48, no. 4: 1052–1062.

Larcinese, Valentino, Leonzio Rizzo, and Cecelia Testa. 2006. "Allocating the U.S. Federal Budget to the States: The Impact of the President." *Journal of Politics* 68, no. 2: 447–456.

Lazarus, Jeffrey. 2005. "Unintended Consequences: Anticipation of General Election Outcomes and Primary Election Divisiveness." *Legislative Studies Quarterly* 30, no. 3: 435–461.

——. 2009. "Party, Electoral Vulnerability, and Earmarks in the U.S. House of Representatives." *Journal of Politics* 71, no. 3: 1050–1061.

——. 2010. "Giving the People What They Want? The Distribution of Earmarks in the U.S. House of Representatives." *American Journal of Political Science* 54, no. 2: 338–353.

Lazarus, Jeffrey, Jeffrey Glas, and Kyle T. Barbieri. 2012. "Earmarks and Elections to the U.S. House of Representatives." *Congress & the Presidency* 39, no. 3: 254–269.

Lazarus, Jeffrey, and Shauna Reilly. 2010. "The Electoral Benefits of Distributive Spending." *Political Research Quarterly* 63, no. 2: 343–355.

Lazarus, Jeffrey, and Amy Steigerwalt. 2009. "Different Houses: The Distribution of Earmarks in the U.S. House and Senate." *Legislative Studies Quarterly* 34, no. 3: 347–373.

Lee, Frances. 2009. *Beyond Ideology: Politics, Principles, and Partisanship in the U.S. Senate.* Chicago: University of Chicago Press.

——. 2016. *Insecure Majorities: Congress and the Perpetual Campaign.* Chicago: University of Chicago Press.

Levendusky, Matthew. 2009. *The Partisan Sort: How Liberals Became Democrats and Conservatives Became Republicans.* Chicago: University of Chicago Press.

——. 2013. "Why Do Partisan Media Polarize Viewers?" *American Journal of Political Science* 57, no. 3: 611–623.

Levitt, Steven D. 1994. "Using Repeat Challengers to Estimate the Effect of Campaign Spending on Elections Outcomes in the U.S. House." *Journal of Political Economy* 102, no. 4: 777–798.

Levitt, Steven D., and James M. Snyder Jr. 1995. "Political Parties and the Distribution of Federal Outlays." *American Journal of Political Science* 39, no. 4: 958–980.

——. 1997. "The Impact of Federal Spending on House Election Outcomes." *Journal of Political Economy* 105, no. 1: 30–53.

Lewis, Jeffrey B., Keith Poole, Howard Rosenthal, Adam Boche, Aaron Rudkin, and Luke Sonnet. 2019. Voteview: Congressional Roll-Call Votes Database. https://voteview.com/.

Lipman, Steve. 2014. "Tea Party Too Close for Jewish Comfort?" *Jewish Week*, June 17. http://jewishweek.timesofisrael.com/tea-party-too-close-for-jewish-comfort/.

Lodge, Milton, Kathleen M. McGraw, and Patrick Stroh. 1989. "An Impression-Driven Model of Candidate Evaluation." *American Political Science Review* 83, no. 2: 399–419.

Lodge, Milton, Marco R. Steenbergen, and Shawn Brau. 1995. "The Responsive Voter: Campaign Information and the Dynamics of Candidate Evaluation." *American Political Science Review* 89, no. 2: 309–326.

Lowi, Theodore J. 1964. "American Business, Public Policy, Case-Studies, and Political Theory." *World Politics* 16, no. 4: 677–715.

Lowry, Robert C. 2015. "Analyzing Campaign Contributions in Context: The Effects of Political Environment and Legal Regulations on Itemized Contributions to Federal Campaign Committees." *American Politics Research* 43, no. 3: 425–450.

Mann, Thomas E. 2015. "Foreword." In *American Gridlock: The Sources, Character, and Impact of Political Polarization*, ed. James A. Thurber and Antoine Yoshinaka, xxi–xxvii. New York: Cambridge University Press.

Martin, Joe. 1960. *My First Fifty Years in Politics*. New York: McGraw-Hill.

Mason, Lilliana. 2015. " 'I Disrespectfully Agree': The Differential Effects of Partisan Sorting on Social and Issue Polarization." *American Journal of Political Science* 59, no. 1: 128–145.

——. 2018. *Uncivil Agreement: How Politics Became Our Identity*. Chicago: University of Chicago Press.

Maxey, Chester C. 1919. "A Little History of Pork." *National Municipal Review* 8, no. 10: 691–705.

Mayhew, David R. 1974. *Congress: The Electoral Connection*. New Haven, CT: Yale University Press.

McCain, John. 2006. "2006 NLC Address." *Engage* 8, no. 2: 46–49.

McCarty, Nolan M. 2000. "Presidential Pork: Executive Veto Power and Distributive Politics." *American Political Science Review* 94, no. 1: 117–129.

McCarty, Nolan. M., Keith T. Poole, and Howard Rosenthal. 1997. *Income Redistribution and the Realignment of American Politics*. Washington, DC: AEI Press.

——. 2001. "The Hunt for Party Discipline in Congress." *American Political Science Review* 95, no. 3: 673–687.

McClosky, Herbert. 1958. "Conservatism and Personality." *American Political Science Review* 52, no. 1: 27–45.

McClosky, Herbert, and John Zaller. 1984. *The American Ethos: Public Attitudes Towards Capitalism and Democracy*. Cambridge, MA: Harvard University Press.

McGhee, Eric, Seth Masket, Boris Shor, Steven Rogers, and Nolan McCarty. 2014. "A Primary Cause of Partisanship? Nomination Systems and Legislator Ideology." *American Journal of Political Science* 58, no. 2: 337–351.

Meffert, Michael F., Helmut Norpoth, and Anirudh V. S. Ruhil. 2001. "Realignment and Macropartisanship." *American Political Science Review* 95, no. 4: 953–962.

Mueller, John E. 1973. *War, Presidents, and Public Opinion*. New York: Wiley.

Mundahl, Erin. 2018. "Could Bringing Back Earmarks Be the Key to Restoring Congressional Civility?" *Inside Sources*, March 20. http://www.insidesources.com/could-bringing-back-earmarks-be-the-key-to-restoring-congressional-civility/.

Nardulli, Peter F. 1995. "The Concept of a Critical Realignment, Electoral Behavior, and Political Change." *American Political Science Review* 89, no. 1: 10–22.

National Conference of State Legislatures. 2018. "State Primary Election Types." http://www.ncsl.org/research/elections-and-campaigns/primary-types.aspx.

——. 2015. "The Term-Limited States." http://www.ncsl.org/research/about-state-legislatures/chart-of-term-limits-states.aspx.

Nelson, Garrison. n.d. Committees in the U.S. Congress, 1947–1992. http://web.mit.edu/17.251/www/data_page.html.

Niou, Emerson M. S., and Peter C. Ordeshook. 1985. "Universalism in Congress." *American Journal of Political Science* 29, no. 2: 246–258.

Nisbet, Robert. 1984. "Uneasy Cousins." In *Freedom and Virtue: The Conservative /Libertarian Debate*, ed. George W. Carey, 13–24. Lanham, MD: University Press of America.

Norpoth, Helmut, and Jerrold G. Rusk. 1982. "Partisan Dealignment in the American Electorate: Itemizing the Deductions Since 1964." *American Political Science Review* 76, no. 3: 522–537.

Norpoth, Helmut, and Andrew H. Sidman. 2007. "Mission Accomplished: The Wartime Election of 2004." *Political Behavior* 29, no. 2: 175–195.

O'Hara, Jonathan. 2008. "Aristocratic and Confederate Republicanism in Hamiltonian Thought and Practice." *Publius* 38, no. 1: 56–80.

Panagopoulos, Costas, and Joshua Schank. 2008. *All Roads Lead to Congress: The $300 Billion Fight Over Highway Funding.* Washington, DC: CQ Press.

Pomper, Geral M. 1977. "The Decline of Party in American Elections." *Political Science Quarterly* 92, no. 1: 21–41.

Poole, Keith T. 2015. Party Unity Scores 35th to 113th Houses [computer file]. https://legacy.voteview.com/Party_Unity.htm.

Powell, Richard J. 2000. "The Impact of Term Limits on the Candidacy Decisions of State Legislators in U.S. House Elections." *Legislative Studies Quarterly* 25, no. 4: 645–661.

Primo, David M., and James M. Snyder Jr. 2010. "Party Strength, the Personal Vote, and Government Spending." *American Journal of Political Science* 54, no. 2: 354–370.

Ragsdale, Lyn, and Timothy E. Cook. 1987. "Representatives' Actions and Challengers' Reactions: Limits to Candidate Connections in the House." *American Journal of Political Science* 31, no. 1: 45–81.

Ray, Bruce A. 1981a. "Defense Department Spending and 'Hawkish' Voting in the House of Representatives." *Western Political Quarterly* 34, no. 3: 438–446.

——. 1981b. "Military Committee Membership in the House of Representatives and the Allocation of Defense Department Outlays." *Western Political Quarterly* 34, no. 2: 222–234.

Rocca, Michael S., and Stacy B. Gordon. 2013. "Earmarks as a Means *and* an End: The Link Between Earmarks and Campaign Contributions in the U.S. House of Representatives." *Journal of Politics* 75, no. 1: 241–253.

Rohde, David W. 1991. *Parties and Leaders in the Postreform House.* Chicago: University of Chicago Press.

Romer, Thomas, and James M. Snyder. 1994. "An Empirical Investigation of the Dynamics of PAC Contributions." *American Journal of Political Science* 38, no. 3: 745–769.

Roper Center for Public Opinion Research. 2019. Presidential Approval. https://presidential.roper.center.

Rossiter, Clinton. 1982. *Conservatism in America.* Cambridge, MA: Harvard University Press.

Rudolph, Thomas J., and Jillian Evans. 2005. "Political Trust, Ideology, and Public Support for Government Spending." *American Journal of Political Science* 49, no. 3: 660–672.

Rundquist, Barry S., Jeong-Hwa Lee, and Jungho Rhee. 1996. "The Distributive Politics of Cold War Defense Spending: Some State Level Evidence." *Legislative Studies Quarterly* 21, no. 2: 265–281.

Schantz, Harvey L. 1980. "Contested and Uncontested Primaries for the U.S. House." *Legislative Studies Quarterly* 5, no. 4: 545–562.

Sellers, Patrick J. 1997. "Fiscal Consistency and Federal District Spending in Congressional Elections." *American Journal of Political Science* 41, no. 3: 1024–1041.

Shelbourne, Mallory. 2018. "Trump Takes Infrastructure Pitch to Ohio as Sweeping Bill Stalls in Congress." *The Hill*, March 28. http://thehill.com/policy/transportation/infrastructure/380707-trump-takes-infrastructure-pitch-to-ohio-as-sweeping.

Shepsle, Kenneth A., and Barry R. Weingast. 1981. "Political Preferences for the Pork Barrel: A Generalization." *American Journal of Political Science* 25, no. 1: 96–111.

Sidman, Andrew H., and Maxwell H. H. Mak. 2006. "Pork, Awareness, and Ideological Consistency: The Effects of Distributive Benefits on Vote Choice." Presented at the annual meeting of the Midwest Political Science Association, Chicago.

Sidman, Andrew H., and Helmut Norpoth. 2012. "Fighting to Win: Wartime Morale in the American Public." *Electoral Studies* 31, no. 2: 330–341.

Sinclair, Barbara. 1995. *Legislators, Leaders, and Lawmaking: The U.S. House of Representatives in the Postreform Era.* Baltimore: Johns Hopkins University Press.

Skitka, Linda J., and Philip E. Tetlock. 1993. "Providing Public Assistance: Cognitive and Motivational Processes Underlying Liberal and Conservative Policy Preferences." *Journal of Personality and Social Psychology* 65, no. 6: 1205–1223.

Skocpol, Theda. 1983. "The Legacies of New Deal Liberalism." In *Liberalism Reconsidered*, ed. Douglas MacLean and Claudia Mills. Totowa, NJ: Rowman and Allanheld.

Sorauf, Frank J. 1992. "Politics and Money." *American Behavioral Scientist* 35, no. 6: 725–734.

Snyder, James M., Jr., and Tim Groseclose. 2000. "Estimating Party Influence in Congressional Roll-Call Voting." *American Journal of Political Science* 44, no. 2: 193–211.

——. 2001. "Estimating Party Influence on Roll Call Voting: Regression Coefficients versus Classification Success." *American Political Science Review* 95, no. 3: 689–698.

Stanley, Harold W., and Richard G. Niemi. 2015. *Vital Statistics on American Politics, 2015–2016.* Thousand Oaks, CA: CQ Press.

Steen, Jennifer A. 2006. "The Impact of State Legislative Term Limits on the Supply of Congressional Candidates." *State Politics & Policy Quarterly* 6, no. 4: 430–447.

Stein, Robert M., and Kenneth N. Bickers. 1994a. "Congressional Elections and the Pork Barrel." *Journal of Politics* 56, no. 2: 377–399.

——. 1994b. "Universalism and the Electoral Connection: A Test and Some Doubts." *Political Research Quarterly* 47, no. 2: 295–317.

Stewart, Charles, III, and Jonathan Woon. 2017. Congressional Committee Assignments, 103rd to 114th Congresses, 1993–2017. http://web.mit.edu/17.251/www/data _page.html.

Stone, Walter J., and Sandy Maisel. 2003. "The Not-So-Simple Calculus of Winning: Potential U.S. House Candidates' Nomination and General Election Prospects." *Journal of Politics* 65, no. 4: 951–977.

Stone, Walter J., L. Sandy Maisel, and Cherie D. Maestas. 2004. "Quality Counts: Extending the Strategic Politician Model of Incumbent Deterrence." *American Journal of Political Science* 48, no. 3: 479–495.

Stratmann, Thomas. 1991. "What Do Campaign Contributions Buy? Deciphering Causal Effects of Money and Votes." *Southern Economic Journal* 57, no. 3: 606–620.

——. 1992. "Are Contributions Rational? Untangling Strategies of Political Action Committees." *Journal of Political Economy* 100, no. 3: 647–664.

——. 1998. "The Market for Congressional Votes: Is Timing of Contributions Everything?" *Journal of Law and Economics* 41, no. 1: 85–114.

——. 2002. "Can Special Interests Buy Congressional Votes? Evidence from Financial Services Legislation." *Journal of Law and Economics* 45, no. 2: 345–374.

——. 2013. "The Effects of Earmarks on the Likelihood of Reelection." *European Journal of Political Economy* 32: 341–355.

Stuckey, Mary. 2015. *Voting Deliberately: FDR and the 1936 Presidential Campaign.* University Park: Pennsylvania State University Press.

Thompson, Joel A. 1986. "Bringing Home the Bacon: The Politics of Pork Barrel in the North Carolina Legislature." *Legislative Studies Quarterly* 11, no. 1: 91–108.

Thorpe, Rebecca U. 2014. *The American Warfare State: The Domestic Politics of Military Spending.* Chicago: University of Chicago Press.

Toomey, Pat. 2006. "Why We Lost." *National Review*, November 10. https://www .nationalreview.com/2006/11/why-we-lost/.

Tufte, Edward R. 1975. "Determinants of the Outcomes of Midterm Congressional Elections." *American Political Science Review* 69, no. 3: 812–826.

Turbowitz, Peter, and Nicole Mellow. 2005. " 'Going Bipartisan': Politics by Other Means." *Political Science Quarterly* 120, no. 3: 433–453.

U.S. Bureau of the Census. 2002. Summary File 3 Dataset. https://www.census.gov /data/datasets/2000/dec/summary-file-3.html.

——. 2011a. Summary File 1 Dataset. https://www.census.gov/data/datasets/2010 /dec/summary-file-1.html.

——. 2011b. 2010 ACS 1-Year Estimates, 1-Year Summary File. https://www2.census .gov/programs-surveys/acs/summary_file/2010/data/1_year_entire_sf/All _Geographies.zip.

——. n.d. Records About Grants, Insurance, Loans, Subsidies and Other Economic Assistance Awarded by Federal Agencies, created 10/1/1981–9/30/2010, documenting the period 10/1/1981–9/30/2010. 116 records total. Accessed March 23, 2012. Data constructed from searching National Archives and Records Administration, https://aad.archives.gov/aad/series-description.jsp?.

U.S. Bureau of Economic Analysis. 2018. "Gross Domestic Product." https://www .bea.gov/data/gdp/gross-domestic-product.

U.S. Bureau of Fiscal Service, U.S. Department of the Treasury. 2019. Data constructed from searching "Award Data Archive," for fiscal years 2011 and 2012. USASpending.gov. Accessed September 17, 2013. https://www.usaspending.gov /#/download_center/award_data_archive.

U.S. Congress. House of Representatives. 2015. *Rules of the House of Representatives.* 114th Cong., 1st sess.

U.S. Department of the Treasury. n.d. Treasury Combined Statements of Receipts, Expenditures, and Balances of the United States Government. 69 documents (1872–1940). Data constructed from searching www.govinfo.gov. Accessed July 8, 2015.

Weingast, Barry R., Kenneth A. Shepsle, and Christopher Johnsen. 1981. "The Political Economy of Benefits and Costs: A Neoclassical Approach to Distributive Politics." *Journal of Political Economy* 89, no. 4: 642–664.

Will, George F. 2006. "A Loss's Silver Lining." *Washington Post*, November 9. http:// www.washingtonpost.com/wp-dyn/content/article/2006/11/08/AR2006110802081 .html.

Wilson, Rick K. 1986. "An Empirical Test of Preferences for the Political Pork Barrel: District Level Appropriations for River and Harbor Legislation, 1889–1913." *American Journal of Political Science* 30, no. 4: 729–754.

Wolf, Michael R., J. Cherie Strachan, and Daniel M. Shea. 2012. "Forget the Good of the Game: Political Incivility and Lack of Compromise as a Second Layer of Party Polarization." *American Behavioral Scientist* 56, no. 12: 1677–1695.

Wood, Gordon S. 2009. *Empire of Liberty: A History of the Early Republic, 1789–1815.* New York: Oxford University Press.

Wooldridge, Jeffrey M. 2002. *Econometric Analysis of Cross Section and Panel Data.* Cambridge, MA: MIT Press.

Wright, John R. 1985. "PACs, Contributions, and Roll Calls: An Organizational Perspective." *American Political Science Review* 79, no. 2: 400–414.

——. 1990. "Contributions, Lobbying, and Committee Voting in the U.S. House of Representatives." *American Political Science Review* 84, no. 2: 417–438.

Zaller, John R. 1992. *The Nature and Origins of Mass Opinion.* Cambridge: Cambridge University Press.

Index

Tables and figures have page numbers in italics.

advertising, 5, 62, 63, 162
Afghanistan, war in, 167n9
American National Election Studies
   (ANES), 15, 28–30, 50, 64–65,
   166n6
American Voter, The (Campbell et al.),
   58
Army Corps of Engineers, 21

bipartisan coalitions, 161
blacks, 66, 67, 70–72, 78–79, *81*
Brat, David, 88
Budget Control Act of 2011, 1

campaign advertising, 62, 63
campaign contributions: defense
   spending and PAC, 112; earmarks
   and, 110, 112; electoral vulnerability
   and, 128; in general elections, 110,
   112; from interest groups, 162;
   legislator and voter ideologies and,

111; pork barreling and, 125–126,
   132; for primary elections, 90
campaign donors: challenger's
   campaign support from, 125–126,
   128; contingent liabilities and,
   105–106; decision-making by, 3;
   elite polarization and, 92; ideology
   of, 111; motivation of, 107;
   party leaders as, 22; as rational
   actors in general elections, 111–
   113, 162; "vote buying" by, 111,
   169n4
campaign fund-raising: challengers
   vs. incumbents, 114; contingent
   liabilities and, 105–106; distributive
   benefits and, 14; distributive
   spending and, 112; by experienced
   challengers, 109, 122; in general
   elections, 109, 112, 114, 123;
   polarization and, 122; in primary
   elections, 90

187

pork barrel: definition of, 8, 42; measures of, 18, 24–26, 31–32, 47–48; public opinion on, 6; across time, changes in attitudes towards, 27, 31, 154; transactional nature of, 158, 162. *See also* contingent liabilities; defense spending; distributive spending

Pork Barrel Politics (Ferejohn), 12

pork barreling process: bipartisan coalitions in, 161; consequences of, 12; costs/benefits of, 6, 13–14, 42; description of, 43; electoral motivation for, 19–20, 24, 132; media coverage of, 63; policy-related goals in, 158; presidential involvement in, 23; voter ideology in, 156

position taking: in advertising, 5; centrist, in general elections, 91; compromise and, 7; vs. credit claiming, 42; definition of, 42; elite polarization and, 18, 62; ideology and, 61; mass polarization and, 7, 42; Mayhew on, 5; partisan response to, 57; by political parties, 7, 61; roll-call votes and, 5; in safe vs. marginal districts, 19–20; in statements to media, 5

positive government, 10, 44–45, 55–56

post-Reconstruction and Progressive era, 45, 47

president, 23, 136, *137*

presidential elections: ANES issue scale during, 29; "conflicted" conservatives in, 60; disasters and, 23, 77; grants, liberalism, and county vote share in, 133; incumbent party, vote share, and results of, 50–51, 52, 94–95, 133

president's party: competitive primaries and, 95–98; credit claiming by, 23; general elections and, *137*; incumbent's party, vote share,

and, 50–51, 52, 95, *137*; in mid-term elections, 136; in primaries, incumbent's party and, 98; productivity and, 160–161; RGDP, incumbent's party, and, 51, 52; voting choices and incumbents from, 79–82; wave elections and incumbents from, 51

primary elections: campaign contributions for, 90; deterrent effects in, 102, 120; encouragement effect in, 3, 102; endorsements in, 92; fund-raising in, 90, 105–106; in homogenously partisan districts, 24; ideology in, 91–95; importance of, 89–91; polarization, pork, and, 92–94; political conditions in, 95–96. *See also* competitive primaries

project grants, 9

public-works spending: ideology and, 10, 167n4; opposition to, 8; polarization and, 15, 153–155, 159–160; study of, 42–56

race: government spending views and, 66, 67, 70–72; voting choices and, 78, 79, *81*, *82*

Reagan era realignment, 47

real gross domestic product (RGDP): competitive primaries and, 95, 97, 98, 99; incumbent's vote share and, 51, 52, 136–138

redistricting reform: competitive primaries and, 92, 96, 97, 99, 100; experienced challengers and, 115, 116, 169C6n5

representatives: behavior of, party influence on, 21–22; casework of, 9, 42, 76; decision-making process of, 13–14; party unity score of, 32; role of, 3, 9, 62. *See also* incumbents; legislators